I0152681

THINK
— AND BE —
RICH

THINK
—— AND BE ——
RICH

AND THE PORTAL TO
FINANCIAL GOLD

ELI SCOTT

Squishy Publishing

THINK AND BE RICH

AND THE PORTAL TO FINANCIAL GOLD

Copyright © 2023 by Eli Scott.

All rights reserved. No part of this book may be used or reproduced by any means, graphic, electronic or mechanical, including photocopying, recording, taping or by any information storage retrieval system without the written permission of the author or publisher except in the case of brief quotations embodied in critical articles and reviews.

ISBN: 979-8-9872-7580-1 (eBook)

ISBN: 979-8-9872-7581-8 (SC)

First Edition.

Squishy Publishing

Squishy

THINK AND BE RICH AND THE PORTAL TO FINANCIAL GOLD

The No Nonsense Book to Personal Wealth.
Follow the Cricket through the money maze to
the pot of gold.

DEDICATION

This book is endearingly dedicated to all of the parents who do everything they do to enterprise their children.

To my parents first and foremost. Thank you for putting up with all of my insanity and lovingly supporting me through all of my endeavors.

To all of my beautiful sisters. Thank you for being so cool and accepting of me, protecting me, and supporting me through everything.

I owe a special acknowledgment to she who took me on this new journey to find all that I desire. I don't think I would be where I am today if it hadn't been for you.

Further acknowledgments go out to everyone who supported me on my path to success.

I couldn't have done this without any of you. You all know who you are.

Thank You.

DISCLAIMER

This book does not provide or guarantee employment, success, or results in any business, career, or investment. Individual results vary. In addition, caution should be taken against risks involved in any business or investment opportunity and we suggest seeking legal, financial, and business consult with any pursuit.

This book is intended for educational and informational purposes only in career and financial wellbeing. You nevertheless need to know that your ultimate success or failure will be the result of your own efforts, your particular situation, and innumerable other circumstances that extend beyond the scope of this book.

The information and/or documents contained in this book do not constitute legal, financial, or investment advice including that of credit analysis and should never be used without first consulting with a financial professional to determine what may be best for your individual needs.

The publisher and the author do not make any guarantee or other promise as to any results that may be obtained from using the content of this book. You should never make any investment decision without first consulting with your own financial advisor and conducting your own research and due diligence. To the maximum extent permitted by law, the publisher and the author disclaim any and all liability in the event any information, commentary, analysis, opinions, advice and/or recommendations contained in this book prove to be inaccurate, incomplete or unreliable, or result in any investment or other losses.

The publisher and the author are providing this book and its contents on an "as is" basis. Your use of the information in this book is at your own risk.

Past performance of investments are not a guarantee of future results. Each investment decision you make should be made in reference to the specific information available for that investment at the time of so choosing as well as under legal guidance and not based on past recommendations.

Making adjustments to a financial strategy or plan should only be undertaken after consulting with a professional. The publisher and the author make no guarantee of financial results obtained by using this book.

This is a work of fiction. Any names or characters, businesses or places, events or incidents, are fictitious. Any resemblance to actual persons, living or dead, or actual events is purely coincidental.

CONTENTS

THE PORTAL TO FINANCIAL GOLD

"The only person you are destined to become is the person you decide to be…" –*Ralph Waldo Emerson*

"The beginning is always today…" –*Mary Wollstonecraft*

If there is one thing that you can have today, what would it be?

No really, I'm asking you. What is it that you truly desire? Is it more money? To be free from a job? To have more time in your life? Or to have your dream car and your dream home? What if I told you that the real secret no one wants to tell you is that anyone can be wealthy. But how could that be?

When most of us think about what rich is, we think of famous people who became billionaires with their billion-dollar fortunes. And when we look for the books and systems about how to become wealthy, we become attracted to "get rich quick" and law of attraction books, Forbes and Inc. magazine, real estate, bitcoin, and cryptocurrency in our endeavors.

What you will find is that the secret to becoming wealthy is not about amassing millions or even billions of dollars to you. Becoming wealthy is also not about being a sucker to any of these other get rich books and systems that may never bring amazing fortunes to you. What if I told you that the secret to getting wealthy starts with the portal to your financial gold?

I had no idea what I would do for a living someday, or what I wanted to be when I grew up as I studied to receive my Bachelor's Degree. Being that I personally couldn't find anything that I wanted to do with this college degree, my future spelled financial disaster. I had no hope in amassing my fortune until a friend took me on a new journey.

I spent the next ten years reading, listening to, and studying the mindsets of various wealthy tycoons. No matter how much I read or listened to wealthy mindset mastery programs, I still found myself coming home every night with no motivation to work at my get-rich systems while allowing myself to be distracted by other things.

I decided to take a couple years off from all of my endeavors and reflect on my procrastination, the failures with my ambitions, and my missing links to my millionaire enterprise. Through this reflection, I had crafted what I call the three golden pillars to bring massive wealth in your life, and this is what I will powerfully share with you in this book.

This book doesn't provide any boring finance or accounting principles. This book is also not about suspending your shopping sprees or not buying your lattes. You also don't need to go through any thirty day or six-week programs to amass your fortunes.

What you will find is that you can start amassing wealth today merely through actions you can take and a few money principles that you can follow throughout your lifetime, and that the key to bringing abundance to your bank account can be found in secret places that we will expose to you.

We will also abound the magical formulas to amass your wealth with Think and Be Rich principles and the easiest ways to get wealthy for you. Through the portal of financial gold, we will follow the tales of those who went from rags to riches as well as the Cricket who masters the maze to his pot of real financial gold.

Why should you listen to me?

You shouldn't listen to anyone. You should not listen to people who just want your money or people who have no money. You should not listen to success coaches who claim they are millionaires when they may not in fact be millionaires or have only made millions by selling hopes and dreams to people.

Additionally, are you going to listen to people who have degrees in money and finance but are dirt broke, or to the key success and insider secrets of real millionaires who have no degree in such? That is up to you to decide.

The material in this book was craftily put together to:

1. Save you time

2. Save your hard-earned money

3. Steer you on the right business or get rich enterprises that can bring you real money

SHOW ME THE MONEY

This book is not about how to become rich with real estate or bitcoin as there are a lot of books on the market about these things already. What sets this book apart is that it is about the fastest and easiest ways to realistically gain personal wealth as touted by experts in the field.

In several of the chapters, there is a section titled **Show me the money** that will exhibit the amount of money you can realistically amass to you throughout your lifetime by following the simple principles in those chapters. We will also display the estimated amount of money that you can save or accumulate with those same principles at the beginning of those chapters.

This book is for anyone who wants insider secrets on how to get wealthy no matter who you are and where you are at in your journey. Although the key for those who will find the most success are those who start early with these wealth principles ahead.

This book is for all who are looking for their financial gold, and this book is endearingly dedicated to you.

So, if you would like to discover the real ways to make money and become that next millionaire superstar, I will take you on your journey through the first portal of financial gold.

It is now the tale of your fortune you see ahead of you that will start you on your wealth journey.

THE TALE OF YOUR FORTUNE

"Never spend your money before you have earned it."

–Thomas Jefferson

In this chapter:

Estimated savings $1500.00 - $10,000.00 or more

The tale of your fortune starts on a journey in which you see a large pot of yellow gold to amass your fortunes. "With only a $19.99 fee, I can get you started on your wealth journey," says this pot of yellow gold. You think that such a small fee is harmless in which you then find yourself dumping your wallet into hundreds of people's wealth systems to find out that there are more brick walls and locked doors guarded by gatekeepers with barriers to your success.

It is at this point that you become hopeless on this journey to manifest your gold when you see a fortune teller ahead of you.

Although you don't believe in fortune tellers, you are curious to see what she can tell you.

With the exchange of a one-hundred-dollar token, the fortune teller agrees to read your fortune.

"I cannot tell you what your fortune is going to be as it relies on your actions you take in enterprising a system. I can, however, tell you the about the tale of the Ripper on your get rich endeavor."

You decide that you don't want to hear about any mystical creatures and continue on your path to mega-rich superstardom.

Much to your surprise, you see that there is a door that is completely wide open, not blocked by any brick walls or gatekeepers to success.

You excitedly run straight through the open door to your pot of gold, but it is none other than the Ripper that you run into on the other side. Because you had already given the Fortune Teller your one-hundred-dollar token, she kindly finds it in her heart to finish telling you about the Ripper.

"The tale of the Ripper is that in which you run into financial doom on your path to get rich success. You felt that these wealth systems would not fail you in which you foolishly spend twenty thousand dollars with no guarantee of any results at all.

Rather than doing what it takes to be successful, you are simply paying into a bunch of other people's get rich books and systems that you think will magically throw money back at you.

'All you have to do,' says these mystical creatures, 'is to work hard for a few years by plugging into our walls and systems that will bring amazing fortunes to you.'

'Additionally, by plugging into these walls and systems, we can automate the process for you taking all of the hard work off of you,' says these mystical creatures."

"What you don't see at first," continues The Fortune Teller, "is that all of these routine purchases get sucked up by a large whirlwind in the sky which eventually touches down into a tornado and drains all of your fortune from you. The tale of the Ripper is that in which you went through this ten-year time warp paying into all of these wishing wells only to have all of your life savings taken from you."

And within a poof, the fortune teller disappears in front of you. It is now at this point that you dwell over your financial doom you ran into when another mysterious white fog in the sky comes to help you in your get rich endeavor.

You can't seem to make out what this white fog is at first, but then it forms into a body of what looks like an ancient scholar who introduces himself as an Old Wise Sage.

"Don't despair as there is another tale in that of the Creeper that can help you in amassing your riches," says the Old Wise Sage.

At this point you are overwhelmed with all of these things you were unaware of in your wealth journey, but you have already had your house and life savings taken away from you, and you now realize that it would be wise to carefully listen to the wisdom that the Old Wise Sage wants to tell you.

"Looking for that pot of gold is not about pulling out your credit card and expecting that all of these systems or investors will magically spit profits back at you."

"The tale of the Creeper is that in which you were unaware of how much effort it would take to succeed in any enterprise. You felt your endeavor would be quick and easy in which you realize it will take a few years longer than planned, at which point a massive amount of work creeps up on you."

"While there are no magic formulas that will break down these walls or grant you your wish, I can give you some golden keys on how to unlock your success. To look for the magical formula that will take you straight to the pot of gold is like looking for something that does not exist."

After listening to this story, you then ask what this whole get rich plan is about. "Good question," says the Old Wise Sage. "It is within the tale of the Creeper that I will continue to enlighten you on your wealth path."

"Getting rich is not about any quick and easy wealth systems but the ten tricks, ten techniques, and ten talents of the trade that you will discover these hidden formulas on the journey to your success."

SHOW ME THE MONEY

"Before I go, there is one more important thing I need to tell you. As you will find out at the end of this journey, it will be highly important to save all of your money from automated systems* as we can show you real wealth systems that can make you money. In these other real wealth systems ahead of you, there are minimum amounts of savings you are required to invest in these types of opportunities which you can lose out on if you waste your money on these automated systems. By not spending your money on these automated systems, you can save between $1500.00 and $10,000.00 over a few years time that you can put into more beneficial things ahead.

A golden key to mastering the road to your wealthy success will be about finding the free resources that can enlighten you. In rising above the picture, I can see all of the people with hearts of gold who can help you on your get rich success.

It is now that I invite you to rise above the picture in discovering these hidden gems in the corners of the maze to your success."

Within a poof the old wise sage disappears in front of you, leaving you to figure out this new path in bringing your fortune to you.

It is with this enlightenment that you rise above the picture to see what it can reveal for you on your wealth path.

KEY TAKEAWAYS

- Your future fortune can never be foretold to you as it solely relies on your actions that you take to amass your wealth.

- Paying into endless streams to automate your business can deplete important savings that can be used for more beneficial investments that carry investment minimums to you.

- The amount of work and time that it can take to become wealthy can creep up on you in which you will still need to learn the ten tricks, ten techniques, and ten talents to your success.

*What is an automated system?

An automated system is any subscription or service that you can pay into to take a routine and time-consuming task off of you. Some examples can be paying into customer support, legal services, payment systems, accounting services, marketing services, ad campaigns, newsletters, emailing systems, etc. A lot of programs and people will bait you into their wealth systems with the idea that you can simply pay into all of these systems that will take all of the work off of you when you can still fail at these money draining systems.

While these can help a business grow, you will need to prove your business venture before paying into these systems which can drain all your money from you.

This will be discussed further in the last chapter, but we now embark on the tale of those who simply get rich ahead.

THE TALE OF THOSE WHO SIMPLY GET RICH

"Our greatest glory is not in never falling, but in rising every time we fall."

–Confucius

You have now learned that there are no magical formulas on how to get rich when you rise above the picture to discover what this get rich plan is about.

This time, rather than seeing any mystical creatures with magical formulas to their pot of gold, you see a Cheetah running in the distance ahead of you. But you notice something different about her in that she is running faster than anyone else to her get rich success. You want to learn how she speeds to her riches in which you run into the Tale of the Cheetah.

You start reading the tale, but then you hear a soothing voice suddenly sneak up on you. You cannot see this mystical woman, but she calls herself the Wind Whisperer as she speaks to you.

"You do not need to read the tale of the Cheetah, as I can tell the story to you.

The tale of the cheetah is about she who runs as fast as she can to her wealth without getting distracted in the process."

"How does she sprint to her destiny?" you ask. "That is a very good question," continues the Wind Whisperer.

"The tale of the cheetah is that in which she will thoroughly research everything and determine that a wealth system is viable (proven and real) before throwing one penny into a wishing well that never spits back money."

"Once she has found what it will take to be successful with a wealth system, this Cheetah will then follow the golden formula to hustle first, find investors or lenders to financially back her, prove her enterprise with the markets, bring in revenue, and then invest her hard-earned money to expand her business as necessary."

"And so, as you can see, those who simply get rich are those who hustle and prove a wealth system. Rather than dumping their money into the wishing well, they dive into the wishing well to become that all-star player who throws tokens at investors who will help them make their business profitable."

"So now why would someone be willing to give money to you?", continues the Wind Whisperer. "As you learn how to win this get-rich game, you will come to discover that investors are willing to invest in you because you are the one who has the smarts and the drive to hustle for them. Investors are busy people too and they throw their money into a wishing well that has an all-star baseball player inside who will aggressively do what it takes to make that transaction profitable. With this, you will see that your success with any get-rich enterprise, whether that of a proven system or that which is based on all wealth, is fully reliant on the actions you take in doing so."

"The golden key to this all-star success, however, is to first determine whether it is something you are passionate about and if you can seek the investment backing and free digital platforms* in doing so."

"There is only one more thing I want to tell you before I go.

Many finance and get-rich gurus predict and guarantee that we will experience another financial collapse in the next ten years and that we will continue to experience cyclical recessions throughout our lifetime. These gurus will tell you that you need a "plan B" or a side hustle** which will give you more security than your one job alone in order to survive another great recession."

"This guru will also tell you that running your own get rich enterprise or side hustle is not a sprint but a marathon. This cheetah is smart enough not to be gullible to the falseness of such claims.

Even if you cannot personally get a job or secure a home at any point in time, these side hustles are not immune to financial recessions and all other market forces that you are up against.

These systems are also not meant to make you rich but for you to hustle someone else's system in which they collect a few thousand dollars from you. Additionally, marathons lead to discouragement and ultimate destruction by these systems that you continuously pay into.

The story of the Cheetah is one in which she sprints through the picture to discover what she is passionate about and goes straight to her destiny without losing any money or time in the process."

And within a poof, the Wind Whisperer disappears in front of you.

It is now at this point that you are wondering what systems these successful people plug into that are tried and true when you see some new pots of shiny yellow gold ahead of you. You run as fast as the Cheetah towards your new found success when a black fog suddenly sneaks up on you, stopping you from moving further. You lose hope on what to do when another mystical creature comes to your rescue.

KEY TAKEAWAYS:

- The tale of those who simply get rich are those who hustle and work hard at proving a wealth system and then finding others who can financially back them.

- Side hustles are not immune to financial recessions and are not always meant to make you rich, especially if you must pay into them.

- The hidden gems in the maze to your pot of gold is about running to many resources in that of books, people, digital platforms, and your inner voice that all carry a wealth of free information.

- Becoming rich is about finding real and viable systems rather than losing out on a bunch of wishing wells that never spit back money.

*What are free digital platforms?

A free digital platform is that in which it provides a free website and free integrations for your business to help you get up and running before you pay any money into it. Integrations are the same thing as automated systems to help run your digital business for you such as ad campaigns, customer support, payment systems, and shopping links for ecommerce stores. One example of a free digital platform that provides these free services with limitations is MailChimp.com.. They provide a free website for only up to so much storage space and amount of customers and not all integrations are free but come with trial periods. It is important to always seek free digital platforms to prove a business before paying into any one else's digital systems, even if they claim to already have a customer base for you. Be sure to read all terms and conditions of any free digital platforms as they can also have other stipulations in using them.

**When side hustles can be beneficial to you:

We are not discouraging you to have a side hustle to bring in extra income to you, but quite the contrary. As we will discuss in later chapters, side hustles are key to paying off debt and increasing your savings and retirement but it is only those side hustles where you are employed by someone to work a system that is already in place, and you are on a regular payroll or working for tips. We would not suggest working for shady systems that are not well established and require your up front investments.

THE TALE OF THE ROAD TO WEALTHY SUCCESS

"Keep away from people who try to belittle your ambitions. Small people always do that, but the really great make you feel that you, too, can become great..." –**Mark Twain**

"Think for yourself, or others will think for you without thinking of you..." **– Henry David Thoreau**

Although, you have made it through this maze to strike gold, a black fog suddenly comes over you. You reach out to your new friends to help you, but to your dismay, you are not finding the Old Wise Sage, the Fortune Teller, or the Wind Whisperer to come to your rescue.

Being left with nothing to do, you magically conjure up the mystical creature of Diary. For a couple of days, you find yourself journaling your thoughts and feelings about what this black fog is that has come over you. In the process, here is what your Diary says back to you:

"When you cannot seem to find the answers that you seek, you turn to me, and I will speak to you. I can tell you about how to break past this black fog that has come over you. You will find that your barriers to success have nothing to do with not being tricked by any of these other misfortunes that you have already run into but breaking past the three barriers that lie within you.

The first barrier is that of sunshine. The second barrier is that of sugar. And the third barrier is that of what you don't think is possible within you. All three barriers paralyze you.

It is within these beauties of sunshine and sugar, romance and rain that we get comfortable and distracted by all of the pleasures that we can give into, stopping us from pursuing our dreams further. Additionally, we wake up to the same ball of fire everyday, filling us with the feeling of who we are supposed to be and what we ought to do. We further have limiting beliefs and people who tell us what we can and cannot do in amassing our fortunes.

When you combine all of this noise with that of a body that gives into the beauties and pleasures in life, we become too comfortable to do in which we are blinded as to what could be real, and we fail to move forward in our passions.

So lucky for you, I have a solution in bringing your fortunes to you. Before you continue your wealth journey, you will see a rustic golden tree ahead of you. When you visit this tree, you will discover that it is up to you to pursue forward regardless of what highs or lows take over you. When you continue your wealth journey, you will see that you have the power to not listen to other people who want to tell you what you can and cannot do. And before I go, I want to present the principle of significance to you.

The principle of significance states that only you determine the path you will take and where it will get you.

And it is with that, I leave you with my final words to do unto you."

With this newfound discovery, you are now starting to understand what stops you from pursuing your gold. Routinely waking up to the same alarm clock, the same coffee, the same job, and the same house every day implant a robotic code into your mind, body, and soul of what you can and cannot do.

And it is now that you have resorted to this Diary that you have realized that this pot of gold is real and that you must do whatever it takes to find it, regardless of how others define you.

It is with this new discovery that this black fog disappears in front of you in which you see the Rustic Golden Tree in the distance to bring an abundance of wealth to you.

🗝 KEY TAKEAWAYS:

- The black fog that can stop you from pursuing further has to do with the barriers that lie within you.

- It is the pleasures in life that can numb and distract us in our wealth path.

- We feel that we are limited by what we can do by the negativity of people around us and defined by our day to day lives in front of us.

- Only you can determine who you are and what is significant to you.

- Journaling in your diary can help bring a wealth of knowledge and foresight to you in amassing your fortunes.

- It will be up to you to see the reality of your financial gold and to do regardless of however others define you in which the Rustic Golden Tree ahead of you will open this portal for you.

THE TALE OF THE RUSTIC GOLDEN TREE

"Our greatest weakness lies in giving up. the most certain way to succeed is always to try just one more time..."

—Thomas A. Edison

"The only time you run out of chances is when you stop taking them..." **-- Alexander Pope**

With your new information on how to make your gold a reality, you now see the Rustic Golden Tree ahead of you in amassing your fortune.

You find yourself lying down in the golden-green grass under the mind-numbingly rustling tree when the soul of the branches speak to you:

"You have now learned about the things that can stop you, but it is me who can enlighten you", says the golden tree.

"The power of sunshine and sugar, beauty and rain do not have to take over you. You can use these same powers to accomplish your fortune.

When you lie on the grass, you can feel my pleasing soul connect to you. It is with my beauty that I will brighten you. With the powers of my branches, I will bring an abundance of wealth and knowledge to you.

It is with this that I now open the next portal to financial gold for you.

When you set out on your path, you ran into these people who told you what it takes to become successful with any path. They had informed you that it will not be quick or easy and that you will need to master the ten tricks, ten technicalities, and ten talents that will bring all you desire.

Although I will not list all of these things here, I will guide you.

The best way to enlighten you with this wealth path is to tell you the story of the butterfly.

The story of the butterfly is that in which he starts out as an innocent caterpillar who wants to learn how to fly. This caterpillar learns that he needs to master these three T's to his success when he sees other butterflies getting shot down by a lightning filled sky. And so rather than go fly into this stormy sky, he rises above the picture to see how to get on the other side of the lightning filled skies.

The secret to your wealthy success will also be about learning the ways of the butterfly to dodge these lightning filled skies to your golden treasures.

And it is with this that I will leave you for now but find your body to absorb into my branches of abundant knowledge in which I will continue to enlighten you."

You become numbed by this new drug of the golden tree, rustling leaves, scrying branches, and electrifying grass, however, this is a different type of paralysis. This is the electrification of enlightenment into these new mystic seas that show you how to get to your path of great abundant fantasies.

You now realize that you must learn these tricks to amass your fortunes, but to your dismay, you can't locate this information anywhere. You are stumped on how to open this new Pandora's box of gold when you come across another man in a nice expensive suit in which he says,

"I can show you how to master the ten tricks to success, however, I charge one hundred thousand dollars for this service."

At this point, you don't know what to do as you don't have this kind of money and don't know where else to go to get this information, when low and behold, another man comes to your rescue. It is an investor named Ted who will show you the think and be rich principles to open this next portal of gold for you.

KEY TAKEAWAYS:

- Rather than letting pleasures in life numb and stop you from achieving further, you can learn to use these same powers to amass your wealth further. Many successful people find the answers and motivation they seek by taking a walk, relaxing in the sauna, or lying in the grass under a tree in which ideas or information come to them.

- You can also learn to let these relaxing things transform you and bring a wealth of abundant knowledge to you.

- As the golden formula states, smart entrepreneurs find investors to back them in which it is an investor named Ted who will pay you to hustle this new wealth system ahead.

THINK AND BE RICH

"The safe way to double your money is to fold it over once and put it in your pocket."

-Kin Hubbard

In this chapter:

The first golden pillar to wealth

Estimated savings $25,000.00

It is now at this point that you become stumped on how to learn the tricks to amassing your fortune without paying a $100,000.00 fee when a man with a golden heart comes to your rescue.

"I can help you to learn the ten tricks of the trade on your wealth path. It is not of the essence that you pay me but that instead, I will pay you. Additionally, I will tell you more than that other man would have told you," says this investor named Ted.

"I still get paid for my services, but you will be my all-star player to hustle this for me, and that is all I ask from you.

In setting out on your quest to learning this game, the most harmful thing you can do is let an entire library of free books fall onto you. What I will teach you is that you don't need to bury yourself under a pile of books but to follow the tactics that I will provide to you.

Before I reveal the ten tricks to you, there's a financial portal that I must present to you.

The quest to learning your wealthy success starts with the tale of the think and be rich formula you see ahead of you.

The only thing about this tale, however, is that it is presented by another man who charges a lot for this show.

But don't worry as I will cover this expense for you. The only thing I ask you to do is to absorb the information and to delve into your new journey of discovery to help you master these stormy seas."

And with the exchange of your ticket, the curtain to this show opens in front of you.

You suddenly see thousands of people in an audience all doing the same thing as you on their path to financial gold. And with the sudden hush of the crowd, a silence takes over the audience in charming delight to the upcoming show.

To much of your surprise, it is none other than the Old Wise Sage presenting the show. Without further ado, he begins to speak to you:

"It is now an audience of ten thousand people I talk to. You have gone on long quests to get here in which I congratulate you.

With your continued effort, I present the Think and Be Rich formula in amassing your fortunes to you.

As simple as it may seem, to think and be rich is not about becoming rich through the law of attraction, thanking the universe for what you have, meditating vaults of gold to magically come to you, or being positive in attracting financial gold*.

Think and be rich is simply to think about it. When you look in the mirror, what do you see? You see that anything that has to do with your finance and money has to do with other people taking your money. So when we talk about think and be rich, it merely means to think about your money.

It is with this that I now present to you the Tale of the Hurricane." And with the opening of the next curtain, you see a hurricane in the sky from underneath you. But you notice something much different about this hurricane in that it is sucking up an accelerated amount of homes and businesses in its path of destruction.

"The tale of the Hurricane", continues the Old Wise Sage, "is that of all of the invisible forces that can financially destroy everything in its path. Within this hurricane, you can also see the Bermuda Triangle in depleting your fortunes."

"The tale of the Bermuda Triangle can be described by an invisible two-bladed propeller that spins in the wind from underneath you in everything that you do. The first blade represents the ten thousand dollars that can be drained from your bank account in a split second from massive debt. The second blade represents another ten thousand dollars that you lose over a ten-year period on hidden fees wrapped up in your finances and loans. The force of both blades combined create a money trap** that drains all of your fortune from you."

It is through your continued effort that we will show you how to preserve your wealth from these invisible forces that take all of your money from you as well as those risky things that can throw wealthy tycoons into total bankruptcy***.

SHOW ME THE MONEY

You have now discovered the first golden pillar in preserving your wealth that you have now saved $25,000.00 in gold.

You don't see or realize this yet as this is not money that you currently have in your bank account, but you had yet to attain and would have had to pay back in debt. It is those who cannot see the true value of what they preserve from these dangerous forces that can be destroyed by this two-bladed propeller that spins in the wind from underneath them.

With this portal to your financial gold, you have now unlocked the ten tricks to wealth that you see ahead of you. The only thing about this tale however is that it comes with a $400.00 fee.

It is up to you whether you want to relinquish this fee, but now you have learned to pick up on some valuable keywords and hidden values to make smart decisions for you.

The valuable keywords to pay attention to is that of real ways to bring money to you. The hidden value is in that of preserving and accumulating wealth. It is with this information that I now leave you to let you continue your destiny."

As the show closes, you decide to contact your investor Ted to consult on this venue in which you open the door to the ten tricks to wealth ahead of you.

🔑 KEY TAKEAWAYS:

- Seeking knowledge on any subject matter is not about getting bogged down in information overload and looking for people who can help you.

- Money can disappear from powerful and dangerous forces that can take it from underneath you.

- These dangerous forces lie underneath every transaction and anything you do where a disastrous hurricane can destroy you.

- The first golden pillar to becoming rich is to preserve your wealth.

- It is with the think and be rich formula that will now open the ten tricks to wealth ahead.

*Some authors like to preach that bringing financial wealth to you is about the law of attraction in praying to the universe, being positive about money, or simply giving yourself permission to be rich. While these things could encourage one to become wealthy, the reality is that financial wealth is simply about thinking about your money, learning what it takes to accumulate new wealth, and taking massive action in bringing amazing fortunes to you.

**What is the money trap?

The money trap is a real concept in money and finance where you can end up paying more in interest than what you originally borrowed on a loan. For example, having to pay high interest or any interest at all can make it take a lot longer to pay off a loan or credit cards in which you can get stuck making endless and unnecessary payments over a period of time. It takes a lot longer to get the principle of the loan down putting you into further debt, hence, the money trap. Others might also define the money trap as trading time for money in which one may never be able to retire. This is also known as the rat race where you are endlessly working long hours to never catch up on your bills and debt.

The best way to avoid the money trap? Don't borrow on credit cards or put yourself into unnecessary debt and look for ways to leverage your income which we will go over in several of the chapters ahead.

***Although some people become massively wealthy from their enterprises, they are not immune to cyclical forces that can still throw them into total bankruptcy. One famous example of this is Donald Trump who became a billionaire and then filed bankruptcy. He was able to become a billionaire again as he had the means to do so, but this is still a good example of how no one is risk averse to market forces with anything they do.

THE TEN TRICKS TO WEALTH

"If we command our wealth, we shall be rich and free. if our wealth commands us, we are poor indeed."

—Edmond Burke

In this chapter:

Estimated accumulation of money

$100,000 -$1 Million dollars ahead of you

You have now come to the Ten Tricks to Wealth formula in your journey in which there is a $400.00 fee.

You remain confused as on whether to pay this fee or look for the free information in the maze to your gold when your investor Ted who paid you to hustle this comes back to help you.

"What you will find on your journey to becoming rich is that there is not one, but two hurricanes that can powerfully take all of your money from you," says Ted. "The first one is that which you see in front of you while the other which lies behind you. It will be in mastering these forthcoming tricks that will outwit these two hurricanes to bring your mystic river to you.

The mystic river is that in which all of the wealth you can have if you follow the wealth principles that we will provide to you.

If you would like to go on a journey to derive this information of old, you are welcome to get bogged down in information overload which can lead you in ten different misleading directions.

Although the $400.00 is still in excess, this is the path could bring you greater success.

You don't have to immediately pursue everything you come across as you can take your time to sleep on it. It is within these mystical inner powers that I leave you to make an educated decision for you."

After a night of rest you decide to pay your $400.00 fee in your determination that these are the systems that are starting to spin your wheel of fortune. With the exchange of your token, it is a Golden Leprechaun who presents the formula of the ten tricks to you. Without further ado, he begins to speak to you:

"Upon your journey to learning the formula to your wealthy success, you will find that there are not ten, but thousands of tricks for you. With so many tricks to discover, you can find them within the entire picture in front of you. It is with this that I now reveal to you a field with other ballplayers. In this distant field to explore, you will see all who throw their pitches at you as well as a cricket accumulating his wealth further. As you can see in this picture, the Cricket is collecting gold nuggets as he hops from corner to corner.

As the Cricket will teach you, the money that will make you wealthy is sitting in the corners of your bedroom.

The formula to get rich is not about buying a pot of gold that is already magically filled for you, but as the Old Wise Sage taught you, to preserve the gold that is right underneath you.

If you don't learn to preserve your current personal wealth, you will forever lose all of your wealth.

As you find out, preserving your wealth does not necessarily mean that you cannot spend money or go on some shopping sprees, but to protect it from certain transactional fees with the five personal finance principles ahead."

SHOW ME THE MONEY

"As these personal finance principles will show you, thinking and being rich simply comes down to not building unnecessary debt as well as avoiding the inflated costs built up in your investments and various financial dealings.

The first personal finance principle is the art of negotiation. In this principle, the Cricket learns that everything can be negotiated when it comes to his money and that he is not illegally or unfairly taking advantage of anyone when he is preserving what is rightfully his. A person can be made to believe that she is solely responsible for paying all costs in a large transaction (think closing on a home) when it can in fact be negotiated on which of the two people fairly takes on these costs. Rather than paying for all costs on a real estate transaction, a wise buyer or seller should obtain a good realtor or lawyer to powerfully negotiate and protect her wealth when the circumstances are in her favor.

The second personal finance principle is to not upgrade or refinance homes or vehicles if doing so can cost you an additional ten thousand dollars in hidden and unnecessary fees or to lose your original down payment of five thousand dollars if the transaction is not in your favor.

With this principle, it will also be important that you understand the total costs of your interest and other fees over the entire life of any of your loans, or hire a savvy broker to help you.

The third personal finance principle is to not spend hundreds of thousands of dollars on expensive schools when a quality education from an alternative school at a fraction of the cost will do, or to find the employer who will reimburse tuition costs to you.

The fourth personal finance principle is to find a wealth manager* who can help you invest in things that can bring residual income back to you. It will be wise that you work carefully with this advisor to make sure you are investing in the best instruments for you with your risk tolerance and to look for investments with fewer fees and higher returns on them. (Please see disclaimers on the front cover).

Furthermore, you can find the qualified brokers who will hustle at a fraction of the price to you versus those who receive high commissions for their services they provide to you. It will be in consulting a qualified tax advisor and lawyer on any of your investments, loans, businesses, real estate, and finances that will only propel you.

And the fifth personal finance principle is to get all of the different insurance packages that you need to protect you in major and supplemental health, house and auto, and business liability. It will be on you to always carry health insurance as doing so can save you another $100,000.00 or more from medical bills throughout your lifetime***.

One final thing to consider is that in a hot selling market where houses practically sell themselves, a highly qualified realtor with only a 1% commission rate will do.

And so now, as you can see, the cricket has learned to master the trade of protecting and preserving his gold and therefore allowing his bank account to continue to grow by not getting suckered into tricky finances.

While we can't give you an exact number on these personal finance endeavors, it is those who follow these principles that can potentially amass an extra one hundred thousand to one million dollars** in wealth over their lifetime. However, if you would like to super charge your wealth success, it will be in the ten techniques and talents to wealth that will reveal more secrets to you.

I leave you for now to embark on this luxurious lifestyle."

Within a poof, the Golden Leprechaun disappears leaving you with a new wealth path and you magically manifest your first nugget of gold with the these first five personal finance principles. You excitedly rush to the bank to cash in what equates to $2900.00 in savings for you.

Although you thought the $400.00 was expensive, you mastered your journeys in seeking the correct information and mind mastery before dumping money into wishing wells that only make you history. Becoming rich is not about throwing your money into wishing wells that don't spit back money but paying the professionals who do real things to preserve your gold and enterprise you.

You haven't been more excited in your life because now you are starting to strike gold when you have now unlocked the next portal to the ten techniques and talents in financial gold ahead of you.

Life Lessons:

I had almost hired a realtor to sell my townhome in one of the hottest selling markets in the world in which she wanted a 3.4% commission rate. A 3.4% commission rate?! A friend of mine balked. Why the H double hockey sticks would you pay *that* kind of a commission rate in a hot selling market where houses practically sell themselves? I took my friend's advice wholeheartedly and enlisted a real estate agent with only a 1% commission rate in which he had also negotiated the buyer to pay for his commission instead of me (which I had no idea was possible) and brought my realtor and closing fees to absolute zero dollars! This realtor and my friend potentially saved me $30,000.00 on the sale of my home!

I also have buyers remorse with trading in a two-year-old vehicle for another under a VIP program in which I really just got duped out of buying a brand-new car and losing out on my original $5000.00 down payment on the first car.

KEY TAKEAWAYS:

- Getting rich starts with the five powerful scenarios in protecting your wealth through negotiation, unnecessary real estate fees and closing costs on cars and homes, seeking a good education from less expensive schools -or- finding employers who will reimburse tuition costs to you, finding the right brokers who will enterprise you, and protecting your assets through insurance packages.

- The path to get wealthy is about finding which systems and professionals (qualified financial brokers, tax advisors, and lawyers) to pay into who will only enterprise you.

- Upon learning of these forces, you are now discovering your mystic river which is all the wealth you can have if you follow the principles we will provide to you.

*What is a wealth manager?

A wealth manager is someone who has the proper financial licenses to help make you money by brokering with institutions and investments that carry low fees and expenses such as index funds whereas other types of brokers may work with investments that research has shown can deflate a significant amount of your investments over a lifetime from excessive and expensive fees. It will be on you to find online calculators that can help you project the total costs of your investments over a lifetime and to seek the right brokers who care to enterprise you in your wealth path.

**Where do we come up with up to 1 Million dollars in estimated savings for you?

This is the estimated savings or growth you can see throughout your lifetime by avoiding medical debt and expensive real estate or fiduciary fees by getting the right protection, brokers, realtors, and lawyers to negotiate for you.

***How to shop for insurance:

As the old saying goes, the best way to shop and compare anything is through third party systems that can provide unbiased information to you.

A good way to shop for a good auto insurance company is not through any quotes that they give you, but by those that only the judicial system recommends to you through their official websites.

The insurance board of your local state or province can also possibly provide information and resources on the best home, auto, dental insurance, and supplemental health packages for you.

Is rental insurance, cell phone insurance, and extended car warranties really worth it? That's for you to research and decide

.

THE TEN TECHNIQUES AND TALENTS TO WEALTH

"Success is the sum of small efforts, repeated day in and day out..." –*Robert Collier*

In this chapter:

Potential savings: Approx. $3500.00.

Potential wealth accumulation: TBD*

Upon plugging into your free resources to determine the ten techniques of the trade, you run into the pathway that will manifest all of your gold. It is upon the guidance of your newfound proven system that you are guided to none other than that of a course in Enterprise strategy, however, this course comes with a $3500.00 fee.

You thought you had found the golden key to unlock this success in which you once again consult Ted on this venue.

"I don't think you need to pay any high fees for this subject matter as there are many schools who provide it for free. In this case, you are only looking for high-level information on how to master the trades. Over time, you will decide which of these more advanced courses you should pay for. Additionally, as you find plenty of different high-quality sources out there, you will discover that you will receive much more knowledge than what this one school has to offer.

In the process of not paying such a high fee, you are now starting to escape the Bermuda Triangle in which you are appreciating the money that you are preserving and allowing it to grow your snowball of wealth further. It is with this that I wish you luck in this endeavor."

And with that, you come across the free teachings of Professor Jack. What you thought would be a boring lecture he presents to you, you see what looks like the journey of a man who walked seven thousand miles in mountainous terrain engulfed in violent storms and tumultuous sea waters.

"I was once a man like you, going on the same journey to my gold," says Professor Jack. "I learned all of the same lessons in rising above the picture to discover my riches. As you have learned on your journey, the trick to amassing your wealth is about looking at the entire picture filled with other ballplayers."

"In this entire world in front of you, you see all those people and enterprises who use thousands of strategies. The tale of those who simply get wealthy is not about those who simply get wealthy, but those who worked hard at building their empires. These were not overnight sensations for these wealthy tycoons but the result of igniting many fires which now brings me to the tale of the magical campfire.

Within this tale, you can see a man out in the middle of nowhere in which he gathers tinder and lights his first campfire. He then continues on his path to gather more tinder and light another fire and then more, which represent all of the land or business he has acquired. After lighting so many fires he then manifests what becomes his wealth empire.

The gathering of your tinder to light your fires is in that of working just as hard at igniting your fires by acquiring the skills and knowledge that you need and then translating it in a way that will amass your fortunes which now brings me to another tale of the Engineer and the Writer.

In this tale, you see a man who sets out on his venture thinking that he is only going to learn Engineering but not Writing, or the woman who wants to learn Writing but not Engineering. As they both travel their paths refusing to learn each other's trades, they go down a very long rough and windy road in which neither one of them learns how to speak to the other or translate their art in a way that the general public can understand or take to heart. The lesson to be learned in this tale is that anything that has to do with making money involves learning technical code and how to translate it in a way that people will want to buy or invest with you. The best way to learn these codes is in the formula of the ten techniques in bringing fortunes to you. Within this tale, you will see that people of all professions must learn these techniques. No matter what it is you set out to do, the following five techniques will enterprise you:

The first technique of the trade is to learn the subject matter in whatever you do. The second technique of the trade is that in which you gather thousands of many individual parts. The third technique of the trade is that you have to learn how to craftily engineer, reverse engineer, build, and unravel your code. The fourth technique of the trade is to then connect all of the parts. The last technique of the trade is to then find out how to masterfully put it all together in a way that sells or steals people's hearts**.

And the final thing that I want to say before I go, is that anything you do involves determining people's wants and needs that all will come to you."

This now brings us to the ten talents in crafting your skills in a way that will manifest your trade in bringing fortunes to you. The tale of the ten talents is not about ten, but hundreds of ways to mastering your trade. While there are too many talents to discover, the golden key is to interweave that of your true passion and crafting your skills in a way that will attract people to you.

SHOW ME THE MONEY

With your continued endurance to preserve your current and future gold, you will find your snowball of wealth to explode.

It is with the planting of your seeds and collecting your tinder that you are igniting your fires to bring your next $10,000.00 to you.

It is not the information that paid you this money but that you found yourself building your wealth in the actions you took and the techniques you pursued to lead you to your wealthy empire.

As you continue to hop from corner to corner or attain a talent to endeavor, you will start to build the enterprise that will bring you all of your treasure.

If you are finding that the ten techniques and talents will be too hard to endeavor, then it will be in the next tale of the easiest ways to get wealthy that will enlighten you.

It is within this tale that you will learn the powerful trick to funnel money into your bank account with pink and blue gold. This may not be the original gold you sought after but it can still bring a luxurious lifestyle that you desire.

It is with this that I wish you well on the enterprises you do."

As the curtain folds to the end this show your head swells in all of the overwhelm of the new information that you learned today, and you are now beginning to understand why an investor would pay you to team up in winning the gold together.

It is with all of your treasure that you now embark on the easiest ways to get wealthy ahead.

🔑 KEY TAKEAWAYS:

- It is important to get all of the high-level free information that you need before you determine if you need to pay high fees for courses from any school. Additionally, getting your information from many resources and schools can give you a much more diversified bank of knowledge than what one school has to offer.

- By not paying into any high-ticket items, you are learning to escape the money trap and preserving your wealth further.

- Getting rich is about lighting your campfires to build your wealth empire.

- Mastering the ten technicalities of the trade is about acquiring the skills that you need in bringing fortunes to you.

- The ten talents to manifesting your wealth involves crafting your skills and practicing your trade in a way that sells to people.

*The amount of money you can make with your skills will be determined by how much you work to convert those skills into sales. Depending on what you do, there are millions of dollars forthcoming in the following chapters ahead.

**These five principles describe the interweaving of all of the skills and talents that people have to master in becoming wealthy which includes learning several different aspects (product knowledge, writing, business, technology, and psychology) and collecting and connecting all of the individual pieces together in that of accumulating

THINK AND BE RICH

knowledge, real estate, or product creation to build their empires. No matter what you do, you will learn how to market to people in a way that will want to buy or partner with you.

THE TALE OF THE EASIEST WAYS TO GET WEALTHY

"Wealth consists not in having great possessions, but having few wants." *–Epictetus*

In this chapter:

The second golden pillar to wealth

Potential wealth accumulation – \$100,000 - \$250,000

It is now at this point in your wealth journey that you have learned about those who work hard to accumulate wealth when the Old Wise Sage comes back to share the next golden formula to you.

"As the tale of the Creeper showed you, the amount of work that it can take to get rich can pile up on you. Rather than working hard to learn and practice the three T's to manifest a pot of gold for you, I reveal the easiest ways to get wealthy ahead of you.

While a lot of get rich systems can be all of these negative things that will most likely never bring fortunes to you, the easiest ways to get wealthy are through residual income and cash flow ahead of you**. You gain these things through accumulating your assets while watching your savings and smart spending (called wealth management) as well as having active and passive income which all bring positive cash flow* to you. An easy way to remember this is to work your A-S-S off-that is, Assets, Savings, Spending to bring fortune to you.

It is with all of these things that you can then funnel money into your bank account through the following three personal wealth principles to help bring a windfall of cash to you:

The first personal wealth principle is to cohabitate with other people. When you do this, you decrease your expenses by at least a few thousand dollars by sharing the mortgage or rental costs with other people. The best ways to do this are to rent out a room in your home or buy multi-unit homes while renting out the other units to the home which can increase your bank account by thousands of dollars. Renting out a room in someone else's home is not necessarily a form of cohabitation to amass your wealth if the homeowner inflates the cost of the rent to you.

The second personal wealth principle is to have monthly income through a job and a real side hustle that pays you. Don't think of online programs where you have to invest any time or money, but those where you work for tips or overtime at an hourly position in more than doubling your bank account for you.

The third personal wealth principle is learn all of the different ways to funnel money into your bank account by avoiding credit card debt, or better yet, the credit card institutions and banks that charge drastic and inflated fees to borrow from them***.

We can also funnel money in by learning what systems you can lucratively take advantage of and how to tap into them without spending any money on them and being smart about what money pits look like and what return you get on them.

Be cautious with being lured by the $300 bonuses you can get from opening bank accounts or applying for credit cards as these may not always be in your favor. You can find articles and calculators online as to what actual benefit you get out of these and the expenses you can pile up in hidden fees and interest rates on debt. Find the ways that you can use these $300 bonuses in your favor with using them towards things that will enterprise you.

It is with all of these things that you can do that you will then discover the second golden pillar in building multiple income streams as we will show you.

Although these income streams may seem like they can never make you wealthy, it is these important savings that can qualify you for other accredited investments in lucrative opportunities ahead of you and what can diversify your wealth basket to help protect you in hard times or down markets.

It is with these golden nuggets that anyone can find their buckets of pink or blue gold. However, if you find that you are willing to work hard at the three T's in bringing greater fortune to you, then it will be in the next tale ahead that will help you to create the reverse whirlwind to bring a wealth of royalties back to you in the tale of the meant-to-make-you-rich systems you now see ahead of you.

It will now be up to you to learn this wealth path that will do nothing but propel you."

With a poof, the Old Wise Sage disappears in front of you leaving you to your next golden treasure.

KEY TAKEAWAYS:

- The formula to funnel money into your bank account is saving and protecting your money and setting up multiple streams of residual income and cash flow back to you.

- Personal wealth principle number one: cohabitate or buy real estate with other people.

- Personal Wealth principle number two: Find a real side hustle that you don't have to pay into and where you are working for tips or overtime at an hourly job.

- Personal wealth principle number three: Funnel money into your bank account by avoiding debt and drastic fees from credit cards and loans.

- Remember that the easiest ways to get wealthy are by working your A-S-S off, that is:

A-Assets

S-Savings

S-Spending

And that A+S+S = Residual income and Cash flow

What is residual income?

Residual income is that in which you bring ongoing monthly or biweekly income to you through both active and passive income which are represented by the following chart.

Residual Income = Active + Passive Income

Active Income	Passive Income
Working a 9-5 Job	Investments in things that pay monthly dividends
Side Hustles that pay	Rental Income
(Working for tips)	Cohabitation
Overtime at an hourly job	Double Income with domestic partner or spouse****

(Active and passive income will be explained further in another chapter for you.)

*What is cash flow?

Cash flow is comprised of anything and everything that you do to funnel money into your bank account in all enterprises and systems under both the active and passive income streams as well as savings, retirement accounts, less spending, bargaining and negotiating (sales, discounts, fees), avoiding loans and or excessive fees to borrow money, not refinancing where possible, free or low cost quality education, reducing interest rates on debt, maximizing tax deductions, and anything else you can think of to increase money to you. So cash flow includes active and passive income as well as wealth management in enterprising you and looks like this:

Active Income + Passive Income + Wealth Management = Cash Flow

Wages, Rental Income, Cohabitation double income, Investments with residual income

Working for tips, Overtime at hourly jobs, High profile careers, Sales and consulting, Business ownership, Bonuses and Pay increases, Savings, Credit card and loan management, Less spending, Hiring brokers and realtors to protect you from predatory fees and negotiate costs for you, Working with an investment wealth manager to enterprise you, All types of insurance, Real estate sales, Car sales, Garage sales (you can continue the list from here).

**What is the difference between cash flow and residual income?

Without resorting to any external resources, cash flow is simply funneling money into your bank account in which you have savings that exceed your monthly expenses in maintaining a positive bank account. Residual income refers to those income streams that bring income into your bank account on an ongoing residual basis (daily, weekly, biweekly, monthly). It is residual income that makes up active or passive income streams in accumulating wealth for you as both wages and investments are residual in bringing weekly and monthly checks to you. The first type of residual income in wages is not automated as it requires your time and labor whereas the second in investments is automated in setting up a system that doesn't require your ongoing time and hustle and brings leveraged payments of lots of multiple sales in bringing a wealth of royalties back to you.

***One way to avoid unnecessary bank fees is to bank with institutions that specifically state that they don't charge any unnecessary or predatory banking fees. Such institutes can include credit unions and new up and coming mobile banking systems.

****A Prenup is For Everyone:

While a double income with a spouse can be beneficial to you, prenups are also essential for everyone.

I debated on whether I wanted to add this last thought on your financial wellbeing regarding prenuptials as other money gurus already tout the importance of these to your wealth folio, however, there are many people who fall victim to the lack of these legal documents in their divorce resolutions and don't give any weight to the necessity of them before getting married to someone.

As a case in point, I had a friend once who had a false belief that these legal documents are only for the rich as he said to me. This couldn't be further from the truth as there are many stories of those who are legally forced to pay excessive amounts of alimony to ex-spouses for what could be a lifetime after the divorce, or give away substantial amounts of settlements from retirement plans and savings in place of the alimony, depending on the laws of the state they are in. In some cases, people choose to stay miserably married to someone for the rest of their lives in order to avoid these hefty payouts. It doesn't matter if you are rich or not, prenups can be essential to the protection of savings and finances of everyone, unless you want to be subject to giving half of your paycheck to an ex-spouse over the course of a lifetime which could add up to hundreds of thousands of dollars.

THE TALE OF THE MEANT TO MAKE YOU RICH SYSTEMS

"Success is not something to wait for, it is something to work for…" *--Henry Wadsworth Longfellow*

You have now learned the easiest ways that anyone can gain personal wealth when the Golden Leprechaun now reappears to tell you about the meant-to-make-you-rich systems that can possibly bring tens of millions of dollars to you.

"It is now upon learning the three T's to the trade that you have learned you must work hard for you money.

No one got rich by plugging into these systems that they think are selling them easy formulas and comprehensive packages that provide them everything they need to get wealthy.

When you are looking for and paying into these systems that promise to build your empire, you are simply paying into nothing more than a hope and dream. No matter what types of full packages that these systems claim they are selling you, there is always going to be a lot more to these enterprises than you ever possibly knew.

What these online get rich packages do not teach you is that when you set out on these sorts of enterprises to try to strike gold, that you are then unearthing another phenomenon I call the Rise of the Titans.

The story of the Rise of the Titans is that of the arrogant man who sets up to open an enterprise thinking that it will put him on top of the world freeing him from his job and making him rich. He then shoots up into the sky thinking that he has struck gold, only to have his entire business overthrown and sunk by an opposing warship on the other side.

The smart and proven entrepreneur would simply not get involved in such failing enterprises but with the real enterprises that afford him the ability to build his ship of gold and sharpen his blades in the process.

The trick to mastering your wealth trade is about which of these wealth systems you should plug into and to cut through all of the noise to get onto the right enterprise. This brings me to the tale of the 1908 man.

The tale of the 1908 man is that in which he got rich off of real and proven systems in where he was not up against the dangers of millions of people throwing their get rich systems at him.

Rather than plugging into all of these systems, you can simply strike gold by mining the lands, being mindful of your money, and selling real information from your own head while getting paid to do so.

So as you can see, the man who gets rich off of his endeavors is not the man who is suiting up in some flashy spacesuit and blindly shooting into the mystical night skies that only paralyze. The man who gets rich off of his endeavors is the one who does something viable (proven and real).

It is with this that I now present the meant-to-make-you-rich systems in that of corporations you see ahead of you.

Getting rich is not about cutting your strings from a secure and stable paycheck but quite the contrary. The tale of those who simply get rich is not about those who do it alone but those who team up with hundreds of people to enterprise existing high paying occupations.

This now brings us to the tale of education systems. Getting rich is not about failing in school to pursue fake or risky wealth systems and it's also not about saving your money from school loans.

Dumping your wallet into an educational institution is about making sure that you are passionate enough to do what it is that you are set out to do before you dump your gold into these wishing wells and furthermore, to define the career and where it will take you before letting it define you. While you can pay for an expensive degree, you can hustle the system and get as much free education as you can until you determine that it is a viable degree and path for you.

It is through our enterprise that we then manifest the Reverse Whirlwind to bring royalties and massive paychecks back to you, however, it is only you who can do what it takes to get there.

It is only you who will find the severe passion in anything that you do and find the fuel of the burning inner flame to keep moving you.

It is those who persevere through this get rich mentality that now brings us to the tale of the highest paid people ahead.

KEY TAKEAWAYS:

- Getting rich is not about paying into systems that only sell hopes and dreams to people, but about having a secure and stable paycheck in bringing residual income to you.

- Getting rich is about being paid massive amounts of money by corporations in doing things that are real and valuable in which you can manifest the reverse whirlwind in bringing a windfall of cash flow and savings to you.

THE TALE OF THE HIGHEST PAID PEOPLE

"When two forces unite, their efficiency double…"

—Isaac Newton

In this chapter:

The third golden pillar to wealth

Estimated Wealth Accumulation Approx. $1 Million per year on average

It is upon discovering the meant-to-make-you-rich systems in that of education and corporations that the Golden Leprechaun reveals the Tale of the Highest Paid People to you.

"The Tale of The Highest Paid People is not about becoming the next Bill Gates or Mark Zuckerberg as there is only an approximate 0.05 percent success rate on getting investment backing on these rare unicorn inventions.*

Getting rich is not about trying to build an entire infrastructure on your own, but to work or invest in companies that have millions of hands to enterprise them. The golden key to this formula is to not to become a lonesome caveman in reinventing the wheel but to team up with other people.

So when other people want to preach that the secret to money is other people's money, the real secret is other people's money and sweat by working in teams- that is time, energy, assistance or hands, management or money, and systems.

The secret to Money is to work in TEAMS:

Time

Energy

Assistance (or hands)

Money (or management)

Systems

The point of making money through teams is not to exploit or take advantage of other people but to simply join systems where millions of people are working to make the enterprise happen or to team up in lucrative investments with other people. Rather than trying to invent and finance alone, you join a well paying corporation or invest into other people's solid infrastructures and ideas. In other words, don't build your own new tech platform and try to sell it to other people but rather invest into other people's well vetted and highly projected tech platforms. And of course never do this alone but with the guidance of a qualified lawyer and broker to help you.

So when it comes to discovering that break out mega millionaire superstar business or enterprise that you want you don't need to come out with anything spectacularly new or unique but to work in existing high paying fields.

Those who find the most success in seeking high wages are those who get paid the most in various fields of healthcare, media & entertainment, national correspondence, technology, engineering, industrial design, advanced innovation and other business systems**. The golden key to this formula is by selling intangible or non physical valuable information in a way that converts into tangible results for people. In other words, smarts and information sells when it can be of high value to people.

⑤ SHOW ME THE MONEY

With all of these personal finance and wealth accumulation principles, you have now preserved a few hundred thousand to a million dollars in savings for you while also planting your seeds to accumulate a projected millions of dollars in residual income and cash flow for you.

The tale of those who simply get rich are those who follow the three golden pillars in amassing wealth and pursuing a diversity of real wealth systems in everything you do. The trick is to not throw your money into any pot that promises to spin your fortunes anew but to pursue all of the ancient wealth systems that are solid and true. It's only when you hustle the system and prove it tried and true that one day a ginormous bonfire ignites in front of you. It is with this that you can find the jobs that can pay you millions of dollars.

It is now up to you to set out on your journey to find your mystic river that you are now on day one of your journey, when you come across another Fortune Teller":

"I cannot tell you what your fortune is going to be in the future as your future is heavily reliant on your severe passion with any enterprise that you want to pursue and the massive actions that you decide to take in life to get there. I can however present our final get rich formulas in the number one secret to wealth and the inside secrets to real estate and online trading ahead."

🔑 KEY TAKEAWAYS:

- The Tale of the Highest Paid People is not about those who strive to become billionaires or come up with new ideas and inventions, but those who become massively wealthy by joining corporations that pay them high wages for their knowledge and production as well as selling information that can be converted into tangible results for people.

- The secret to making money is not only other people's money, but other peoples time and hands or to work in teams.

  That is other people's:

T – Time

E – Energy

A – Assistance or Hands (building and running the business)

M – Management or Money (Investments)

S - Systems

It is realistic to strike one million dollars as you start out in these enterprises, but it will be on you to pursue them further.

*What is a unicorn invention? Without resorting to other resources, a unicorn invention is one that is rare or hard to discover and falls under the 0.05% of ideas and inventions that get investment backing by venture capitalists. Most of the founders of these successful inventions build the prototypes on their own and gain traction on their product before any venture capitalist will back them. Some examples of these types of inventions are Facebook, TikTok, and Airbnb among others.

**Some get rich gurus preach that you don't get rich by getting good grades in school, but this can not be further from the truth. There are many people who make millions of dollars a year after having received a good education in lucrative career paths that can turn them into millionaires. Others become rich through avenues that allow them to become national TV correspondents or CEO's of technology companies. We find ourselves looking for all the ways that people get rich with real estate and cryptocurrency while ignoring the likes of Anderson Cooper, George Stephanopoulos, Kelly Ripe, Ellen DeGeneres, Ryan Seacrest, and Tim Cook, an ex CEO of Apple. And while Tony Robbins never attended traditional school, he read over 700 psychology books to build his wealthy empire in life and business coaching.

Other people who become massively wealthy in these avenues are those who start movie production companies such as Dwayne Johnson aka the Rock, Adam Sandler, and Jennifer Lopez who all have reported net worth's in the hundreds of millions of dollars.

Finally, one cannot teach that you simply get rich by ignoring traditional schooling and simply going into wealth enterprises such as real estate when these types of endeavors carry a lot of risk and a lot of work on your part to make it work for you in which you don't find any passion in doing so. Even real estate gurus had to learn a lot of the ropes in what works and what doesn't before they could become successful.

It is not always necessary to get a full bachelor's degree if the high paying careers you seek don't require them in which you can look into certificate programs and trade schools. As some employers will tell you, at the end of the day, hands on experience will be more valuable than any college degrees.

While a bachelor's or master's degree is not required to become a small business or digital franchise owner, it would be beneficial to delve into certificates or specializations in entrepreneruship, product development and management, innovation, business foundations, marketing, and mini MBA or MBA certificates to help you in what you don't know in business formation including minimum viable products, legalities, and market research.

THE INSIDER SECRETS TO REAL ESTATE AND ONLINE TRADING

It is at this point in your journey that your head swells in all the information you learned to manifest your pot of gold when you now come across the tale of those who fail in their get rich systems.

In starting this path to your gold, we will look at various get rich systems in real estate, Non fungible tokens (NFT's), fintech, cryptocurrency, affiliate marketing, e-commerce, and franchising along the way.

Why is it important to embark on this golden key on your journey?

Because a lot of us get swooped up in all of these different types of systems in an attempt to get rich only to find yourself sitting on these ideas never to make anything happen with them when you find no passion or drive in pursuing them. And so when we look for that one missing piece that can realistically make us wealthy, we can start with the most highly touted wealth system in that of real estate and ask ourselves,

If real estate is that easy, why doesn't everyone just become rich with it? And what is the secret to it?

When many of these wealth systems like to claim how easy and simple their wealth building programs are, they fail to disclose the grueling and extensive hustle involved as well as your passion and desire in pursuing them.

Specifically, real estate involves hundreds of strategies and scouring thousands of markets to find something profitable. You may also have to rely on the hustle of other people and finding co-investors who carry the same mindset as you to be successful. While there is proprietary software and automated systems to help you, it will be up to you to determine your drive in pursuing them.

Additionally, real estate buying and investing can be very risky as it is impossible to predict and has been known to throw even rich people into bankruptcy. Finally, you never know when laws and regulations or HOA's can ban your investment opportunities (think vacation and short-term rentals) that can make some of your money making opportunities fail. And while I'm not qualified to speak on digital printing of homes, it will be a matter of time before we see what these will do to the real estate market.

So, what is it that we don't know about making money in real estate?

As rich tycoons will tell you, they make their fortunes not on *one-time* sales of real estate or investments (called an asset) but through monthly or ongoing residuals of income and investments (think payroll and rental income).

So, this all now brings us back to passive versus active income. Active income is described as that where you have to work a lot of hours everyday at a payroll job to see a tiny paycheck with all of the work that you do and you get one paycheck for this job. Passive income is the opposite where you set up one or many streams of income to come to you with little effort on your part to receive large residual monthly paychecks for having done very little for it. The same thing is true in real estate. You can either hustle and work long and hard hours to receive a small sum for all of the work that you do (called active income), or you can set it up so that you invest in units that can bring monthly residuals back to you with little to no effort (called passive income).

So, while get rich books want to preach about making passive income in real estate, it's the type of real estate you get into that will determine the active or passive side of that income stream for you. In other words, flipping homes and real estate brokering are active and not passive income as you have to work your butt off for a one-time asset of money to come to you.

Rather than going through the grueling hustle of these types of systems, real estate tycoons get rich off of passive streams of income through education franchises and real estate investing.

So how should you invest in real estate?

While I am not qualified to advise on how to invest in real estate property, REIT's, or crowdfunding, the only thing I can say is to never do so without speaking to qualified brokers and lawyers with the correct financial licenses who can assess the best opportunities for you and who can help you with this avenue. Additionally, you have no control over the types of real estate that crowdfunding managers buy or the investment strategies they chose, and your money can be locked in for long periods of time all of which can make these types of investments risky.

What about affiliate marketing, ecommerce and franchising?

While I don't think it's necessary to go deep into the pitfalls of affiliate marketing, I will say that it is not generally a one person show and is met with the highest success by big companies who hire teams to make these types of programs profitable.

Affiliate marketing can become very grueling if you are doing it alone in which you have to be able to have a lot of product knowledge on any one of the products that you are marketing, and additionally, you have to constantly remain in strict compliance with the terms and conditions of each of the affiliate marketing partnerships that you sign up with in order to remain profitable.

You also have to maintain highly captivating blogs, marketing materials, and updated and live contests to draw consumer attention. Don't forget the potentially ten or more websites you must also host to be successful.

While I don't want to give advice on digital commerce, consider how one of the largest retailers in the world could not even compete in this realm, losing approximately one billion dollars in one year to their competitor. Ecommerce is also not a one person show in which you can wear the hats of one hundred people and pay into hundreds of systems to make your business profitable.

Any franchise you go into requires yet again a lot of your hefty and endless reinvestments in which it can be difficult to see any profits.

And as some laundromat and franchise owners may tell you, making $24,000.00 a month at their lots is not passive but active income in which they are also working long hours every day to keep their business going.

It is always advisable to scout the people who have success or to get professional consults to see if these types of enterprises are viable for you (and of course to be aware of the up front and ongoing investments and long hours!).

The same goes for coaching businesses which require you to spend countless hours marketing your business and then spending tens of thousands of dollars to buy into someone else's certificate and marketing material to become a coach with their wealth system.

Now am I telling you not to do a consulting or coaching business? No. What I am saying is to know what you are getting into before dropping thousands of dollars into it.

What's Up with the NFT Craze?

It has been reported time and time again that home ownership will be a thing of the past for most adults as we continue to experience the widening gap in wealth between the rich and the poor as well as this current gold mine we are in with everyone buying up real estate in droves to take advantage of the market.

If real estate and retirement plans are no longer the answer, then what is? In an ever-changing world with rising inflation and plummeting investments, it can be so easy to fall into the latest get rich trends in digital currencies to amass a vault of wealth to you.

But what is it about these systems that don't bring amazing fortunes to you?

While we will not go over what cryptos, blockchains, fintech, and NFT's are or how to trade on them as there are thousands of books and courses already, we can briefly discuss some things you should know in pursuing them. Digital currencies may seem like the solution to the future, but there are still many barriers to its massive success and may just be another in and out fad of the past. Think about it, we didn't start this chapter with what is up with the cryptocurrency or bitcoin craze. Although those were the buzzwords within the past five to ten years, they have already been faded out with NFTs. Before I list out some of the barriers to their success, I will mention that fintech (financial technology) includes lending, crowdfunding, insurance tech, real estate technology, Defi (decentralized finance), and anything else to do with financial technology.

Although there are people who claim to make tens of thousands to even "millions" of dollars on these currencies, there will always be more barriers to these get rich systems.

While we do encourage you to research these wealth systems yourself, here's a few things to know about them:

- They are not quick or easy

- They don't come cheap

- They are known to be highly risky

It was reported recently that even one of America's multi billionaires lost out on defi (decentralized finance) opportunity when his investment plummeted to zero in one day in which his sage advice was to be aware of how risky defi can be in which you should highly vet the people who manage the business opportunity. Of course, that billionaire is Mark Cuban and he also suggests to always do your research. And while some people claim to make $80,000.00 a month in cryptocurrencies, financial experts warn of the high risk of these currencies, one of the biggest being that they are not well regulated in which they do not guarantee long term results.

Mining cryptos requires buying expensive equipment (or making your own) to do so and then racking up steep utility bills while spending weeks and months mining for them. In the end, you may spend more money on these electricity bills than what you ever make back on them.

So, then what about NFT's? These fintech tokens can also rack up hefty expenses in what are called "gas" fees to share and auction them. And while you are paying for the gas to share them, there's no guarantee you will make good money on them.

While I'm not discouraging you from these fintech systems, there are calculators and software out there to help determine if it will be worth the cost to extract any of these cryptocurrencies and NFT's. And if you can find the platforms to share your NFT's at low rates then more power to you. But keep in mind the disadvantages you are up against with these platforms that can make it difficult to leverage money to you. Finally, don't forget the taxes you will need to pay in any of your successful profits.

So, what is up with all the hype of people wanting to sell you investment courses with the potential to make you massively wealthy? These are people who are making money by selling these education or consulting systems and not necessarily on these investments that are known to be risky (and that they themselves can still lose out on). At the end of the day, there is no magic formula to successfully trade on any of these investment paths.

The same holds true for all of these gurus who want to bait you into their seminars to retire in 3-5 years with their real estate investing systems. Most of the time, these are gurus who want to charge you tens of thousands of dollars with their get rich systems to learn how to retire in a short span of time with real estate when the reality is that you don't need to spend this kind of money to learn these strategies. Other times, these are recruiting programs for them to build their real estate teams in hustling a system. There's nothing wrong with joining these types of teams as long as you have the passion and energy to work these systems.

On a final note, if you are going to play the lottery, then be willing to learn the skills of those who figured out the secrets to picking the winning numbers. Know that this isn't an easy thing to do either and can take a lot of time and hustle to figure out the probability of these numbers over many months and years in which I find myself going back to the things I care about most. I feel as though I have in a sense won the "lottery" many times in my life in ways that increased my savings by a couple hundred thousand dollars and another projected 1.5 million dollars ahead. With anything you set out to do, you will need to find the "what's in it for you" as we will go over in another chapter.

So again, what is the secret to wealthy success? It will be in the next chapter that will dive deep into building your multiple income streams in active and passive income and your biggest assets ahead that will open this Pandora's box for you.

Caution:

What should you always do before starting any franchise?

Receive a business consult and have all contracts reviewed by a lawyer.

Life Lessons:

Watch out for the programs that charge you thousands of dollars in earning their certificates in coaching or education programs. I have personally been duped out of $4500.00 on one of these coaching certificate programs in which I still had to pay into a website, marketing, and ad campaigns in addition to hustling the business. Also, some of these coaching certificates may still require that you spend over $100.00 per month to stay certified with them or for subscription services to use their informational material in order for you to run your business.

Additionally, these programs don't provide you all of the other systems that you might need such as buying or renting office space somewhere, establishing your online presence, or forming your legal corporation if necessary.

On a side note, if it's only a certificate you are looking for, there are reputable schools who can certify you for these same qualifications if not better for as little as a few hundred dollars.

Another Life Lesson:

I once lost five thousand dollars in three days on an investment that I didn't know anything about and without the use of a professional broker.

KEY TAKEAWAYS:

- People don't get rich in all of these wealth avenues in real estate, fintech, and NFT's due to the ebb and flow of the markets, high risk, grueling hustle, and high expenses in doing so.

- Hustling at any of these wealth systems will require your passion in pursuing them.

- Rich people get rich by selling education and courses to people and investing in things that can set up passive income streams which we will go over in the next chapter.

THE INSIDER SECRET TO BUILDING WEALTH WITH ACTIVE AND PASSIVE INCOME

It is now through these final chapters that we will go over some hidden gems in building your entire wealthfolio (money portfolio made up of savings and assets) for you starting with active and passive income ahead.

As stated previously, those who simply get rich do so not from one-time sales (called assets - think flipping homes) but through ongoing residual income. Rather than going through the time-consuming grueling hustle with flipping homes or running franchises, they look into passive assets and investments that automatically pay them without their active involvement in a system. Additionally, active income allows for cash to flow out of your bank account at a faster pace whereas passive income allows cash to flow into your bank account at a faster pace.

It is with this that I now outline the difference between how money can flow in or out of your bank account with active and passive income through the following diagram:

Active Income	Assets
H	H
Cash Flow	Passive Income
E	E

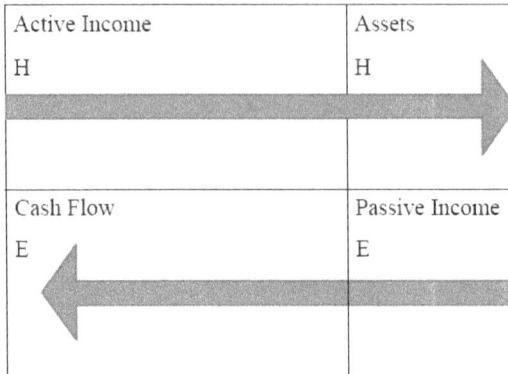

1. The hustler, money funneling out of bank as active income is paid out.

2. The entrepreneur, passive income streams established with residual money automatically funneling into bank account.

As these diagrams show, cash flow can become negative when we have to trade a lot of time for a one-time paycheck (known as the hustler) or positive when we set up ongoing income streams that require little to no effort at all (commonly known as the entrepreneur*).

This chart is not meant to discourage you from working at a 9-5 job or career as both types of income streams can bring positive residual (ongoing) income, which is the most important for building retirement and savings, as well as money needed to fund your passive investment income streams which we will go over in the final chapter.

So while cash flow can become negative through active income streams, residual income remains positive with both as the following chart shows:

Active Income	Passive Income
Negative cash flow	Positive cash flow
Residual income	Residual income

It is with this that we now see it is both active and passive income streams are necessary in building your entire wealthfolio.

And why is that? While some experts tout that no one becomes rich by working a 9-5 job, it is the consistency of residual ongoing income that is necessary to pay bills and debt while accumulating precious savings. These precious savings can then be used for then investing in passive investments to you. And it is both active and passive income that will build multiple residual income streams to pad your entire portfolio for you.

Additionally, it is in high wage fields can bring massive positive cash flow depending on how you manage your money and your individual financial circumstances.

Now wait a second? In some places I am saying not to hustle and in other areas I'm saying to do. What I'm saying is to only hustle for a short period of time in order to build passive income systems and that you will still need to have an income somewhere while building those passive streams of income. Don't hustle at the things that are up against many barriers to success or those that force you to become a slave worker in flipping homes or owning a franchise for the rest of your life.

The main purpose here is to simply show the importance of building passive income streams while working at the jobs that can still bring in ongoing residual income to you.

So what types of businesses or investments are real systems for setting up passive streams of income to you? In my non professional opinion, there are only a few, and none of them are guaranteed to bring positive results. With any endeavor or investment you get into, it will be on you to continue seeking consultation from qualified experts who truly care about you and can help you.

The only types of enterprises that I am aware of that can bring true passive income back to you without your constant effort and grueling hustle are those in passive investments. Think rental income, senior housing, and investments that collect monthly dividends (payments back to you).

Any other types of "passive income" businesses that are not true passive income are those that require your constant hustle and are therefore active income enterprises.

Other enterprises that can set up passive income streams (with up front hustle) are digital franchises and businesses such as books, software, or informational pieces you can sell to people.

It is within these types of systems that carry the least amount of overhead and cost of goods sold*** with the highest profit margin in bringing passive income to you.

It is within the following active and passive income charts that show the different types of careers and other things you can do in bringing fortune to you:

Active Income	Passive Income
Working a 9-5 Job	Real Estate Broker, Flipping Homes, Apartment Complex Ownership
	Multi Level Marketing (MLM), Sales, Consulting, Coaching, Franchising

In this chart, I first show what most people would exhibit to fall under active and passive streams of income in franchising or owning businesses, sales or consulting, flipping homes, real estate brokering or affiliate marketing as well as owning and running laundromats with the bait that you are setting up passive streams of income for you to make you rich.

However, most of these businesses as well as traditional high paying careers fall under the active income category and therefore, the active versus passive income chart looks more like this:

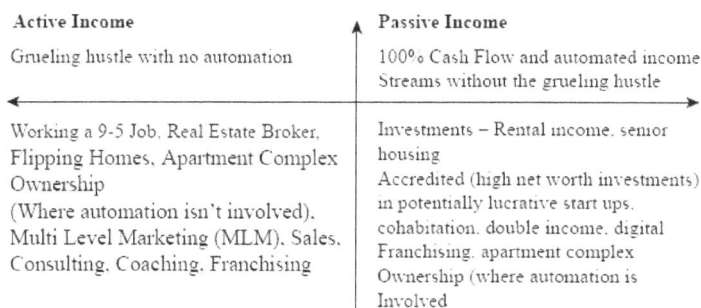

Active Income	Passive Income
Grueling hustle with no automation	100% Cash Flow and automated income Streams without the grueling hustle
Working a 9-5 Job, Real Estate Broker, Flipping Homes, Apartment Complex Ownership (Where automation isn't involved), Multi Level Marketing (MLM), Sales, Consulting, Coaching, Franchising	Investments – Rental income, senior housing Accredited (high net worth investments) in potentially lucrative start ups, cohabitation, double income, digital Franchising, apartment complex Ownership (where automation is Involved

While others want to tout that these are smart passive streams of income, they actually fall under active income in your round the clock effort to keep making money at them (thus no automated systems in bringing passive income to you). In reality, the only smart passive income is either again these direct investments into those that other people are already enterprising and doesn't require any of your attention, or those which only require little effort up front to then turn into passive income streams later down the road (automated systems turned into automatic income).

Now this is not to be confused with thinking that these systems are not lucrative for you. Some of these wealth systems can be very lucrative.

I am only saying they can be considered active income in hustling them to bring income to you.

While we are talking about negative cash flow and passive income, it will be important to talk about automated business systems that can increase or drain your fortune.

When should you buy into automated systems to create passive income?

So what is up with the myth that you can simply pay into automated systems to work your business for you so that you can retire or only work four hours a week?

The reality of automated systems is that they can either create a whirlwind in draining your money and savings and therefore funneling money out of your bank account, or, they can create a reverse whirlwind in bringing a wealth of royalties back to you as displayed in the following diagram:

Automated Systems

The whirlwind of draining all your money from you

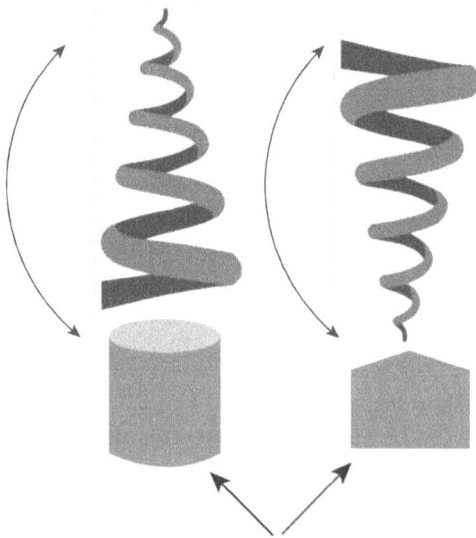

Draining all of your money from you into a sinkhole vs the reverse whirlwind to bring money back to you (into your home).

The first diagram represents that in which automated systems can drain all of your money (and therefore, going down a sinkhole) if you don't prove the golden formula first to hustle first, find investors or lenders to financially back you, prove your enterprise with the markets, bring in revenue, and then invest your hard-earned money to expand your business as necessary.

Whereas the second represents a whirlwind of fortune to come back to you (and therefore funding your house and lifestyle) if you do follow the golden formula to prove the business or wealth system first.

As previously discussed, automated systems are only beneficial in enterprising a business for you when you have first proven a viable and real business and gained traction on the business. A good way to gauge this is to not pay into any of these systems until you have received your first paycheck on the business. A good starting income should be a minimum of $10,000 before paying into systems to leverage your business for you.

So while automated systems can spell financial disaster for those who don't do, they are essential in bringing wealth to those who hustle and prove their get rich system by leveraging services to build passive income streams for you.**

While it is great to know how to build your wealth through these income systems, one cannot truly embark on careers or businesses to enterprise them until they have found their passion and why in pursuing their wealth path. It will be in the golden formulas on finding your why that will help you with this part of the maze to your success. However, we will start with finding your true self in order to find your drive in pursuing your wealth in the following chapters ahead.

Life Lessons:

I once lost ten thousand dollars in three months paying into ad platforms to boost an online business in what was not proven to be a solid business that anyone would buy into.

🔑 KEY TAKEAWAYS:

*   The only types of real passive income that don't require your grueling hustle are those in passive investments.

*   Most franchises and businesses such as running a laundromat falls under active income.

*
    Both active and passive income will be necessary in bringing in residual income to put towards your passive income investments.

*   You must prove a system with as little investment as possible before paying into automated systems.

Caution:

When should you buy into automated systems?

When you have received your first paycheck of $10,000.00 and having a handful of clients.

*Entrepreneur is defined for purposes of this book as anyone who hustles to build their own personal wealth system in any number of passive income streams.

**At the end of this book, there is a reference guide on how much money you should spend on any certificate or automated systems.

***What is cost of goods sold? In layman's terms, cost of goods sold is essentially that of the cost of storing and selling physical products as well as the losses incurred on those that are not sold. And so those who seek to become wealthy by selling hard physical products are up against these costs and losses and in many cases, low profits. It is more advisable for the average person to join corporations and teams or to invest with those companies rather than to try to invent or sell on their own. These types of businesses also have overhead (expenses to keep the business going in utilities or hiring people from underneath them). For the average person, this just isn't always feasible in which they may find more success in higher profits of digital systems where there is no loss incurred on physical products and no or low overhead. This is why some find massive success by imparting valuable knowledge that can then turn into tangible results for people.

THE NUMBER ONE SECRET TO WEALTH

"Educating the mind without educating the heart is no education at all…" *—Aristotle*

So why don't get rich schemes make you rich? There are many reasons why get rich enterprises and businesses fail, and while I don't feel that any one of them are more prevalent than another, I would like to discuss the personal aspect as to why people fail in many business enterprises.

In my opinion, one of the biggest reasons for failure at any enterprise you will attempt is that it WILL NOT BE FULFILLING to you and YOU WILL NOT CARE ABOUT IT.

As the clichés goes, when you think you can or can't you are correct either way-HOWEVER- the difference is in what you are motivated to do.

Unless you CARE about whatever schooling, business or million dollar business you are working on, you will likely not succeed. And why is that?

If your only goal at working at some enterprise is to become rich, you will severely fail because the goal of becoming rich will not be fulfilling to you.

For example, you might find yourself saying I don't care about investments. I don't care about real estate or ecommerce. I do not care to sit at my computer forty hours a week around my job to learn coding or affiliate marketing. And forex is so awful boring that it makes me fall asleep anytime I try to sit through it.

Even though these enterprises have potential for making me a lot of money, I cannot suffer through hustling at these enterprises that I have no passion for!

So no matter how bad you want that dream home or that dream car, if you don't care about something, you are not going to work at it and no dream is big enough to make you hustle at unfulfilling enterprises that do not motivate you.

As a case in point, there are many successful people who admittedly fail in their career aspirations at the most prestigious jobs in the world due to having no passion and heart in solely chasing after money. If we chase after things without knowing our why or what fulfills us with it, we can feel empty inside. When it comes down to it, there is only one thing that drives us with any enterprise, and that is heart.

So when it comes to finding your get rich avenue, you need to do something that you care about.

This is what it takes to be explosively successful at any business enterprise, period and you are not going to have the drive to be successful in life until you are moved by it.

It will be in the burning flame of what you want to do that will carry you through and give you the fuel you need to build your wealth empire.

And once you've found your fierce passion and reason for doing whatever you set out to do, nothing will stop you from doing everything it takes to enterprise you.

Once you find what is fulfilling to you, you will then work eighty hours a week for the next twenty years at the things that matter to you most.

If you don't think that this is important to finding motivation at becoming rich, then let me ask you if you are hustling at building you wealth empire or do you find yourself procrastinating from working at those things that will bring you that success. And furthermore, do you find yourself to be too busy with the things that won't get you there?

If you find yourself saying yes to the last question then it is time to start finding your passion in pursuing your wealth through discovering your true self. As silly as this sounds, we find ourselves grinding away at jobs that we hate or chasing after money at the wrong things for the wrong reasons and failing at our aspirations.

So how do we determine and follow our true self? By not listening to others, not letting others define who we are, and finding our why through the practice of love and self care.

Love and self care is key to everything in your life, from your mental and physical health, to the direction of your future, to the decisions you make, the people you will have around you, where you will live, where you will work, to finding that luxurious home and life within listening to your true self and your true heart that will arouse your passion and allow you to pursue what you do.

When you learn to love and care for yourself, you will start to learn that you no longer have to be obligated to that ball and chain, one hundred per hour work week job. Day by day, you start to build an immunity to your job, and then suddenly, the urge to quit and go find that job that fulfills you (of course I'm not telling you to just quit your job before finding another lucrative one to pay your bills for you). You will also be able to get rid of any relationships that are of no benefit to you.

By arousing our true selves, we can then discover what our purpose is and what we are passionate about or the "what's in it for me".

Now you might be saying that you are already following your heart or that you already know who you are, but if you are still finding yourself to be unhappy, miserable, or confused in your life, or failing at finding success with a chosen career path, I encourage you to seek finding your heart through the power of finding your true you. It is when you do that all will come to you.

Still don't think this is important? Then continue to be broke and miserable. It's your life, not mine. It wasn't until I found my true self that I was able to break free from the golden handcuffs of working at a J-O-B (just over broke) and finding my luxurious lifestyle. How did I arouse my true self? By not letting anyone else tell me what to do which allowed me to release all of my obligations and let go of the things that were not furthering my goals. It was upon my journey in quitting my job and selling my house that I went on a path to arouse love in my heart and finding my why in amassing my wealthy fortune. Although I also had a lot of savings built up from my career and real estate that allowed me to do these things.

In the process of arousing your true self, you do not want to get these things confused with what self care is not.

Self care is not: eating your favorite junk food, drinking that bottle of booze, chronic vices, shopping sprees, drinking that latte, rewarding yourself with gifts, or watching TV or playing video games all day. While I'm not discouraging you from these life pleasures, self care is about taking out time for ourselves and nourishing ourselves on all levels in family, relationships, community, sunshine, air, hobbies, activities, healthy non drug related recreation, healthy non drug or booze related relaxation, sports, and companionship in arousing fulfillment in our hearts.

Self care is about bringing all areas of your life into balance in that of family, friends, physical and spiritual wellbeing which then arouses mental and emotional health, and subsequently more peace in your mind and heart. We seek self care by listening to our inner being as to who we truly are and what we want. And how do we do that? By taking time out for yourself, finding your passion and your why, and doing all sorts of activities that will bring fulfillment and abundance in all areas of your life.

In arousing this knowledge, what is self care to you and how would you define it? What activities can you do to release your mind and find fulfillment in your heart be it in any of these activities?

Take it upon yourself to spend no less than one hour a day every day for the next seven days* to practice any form of a self care activity of your choice and while you do, hone in on your true self and reflect on how you feel and what you discover about you.

When resorting to any of these self care activities, how do you feel, do you feel relaxed, rejuvenated, and energized? Do you feel happy, in a better mood, and finding that you are getting more restful nights? How can these things help you to find wealth in your life, be it heart wealth or money wealth? In this process, do you find that you are releasing yourself of unnecessary obligations or letting go of things that aren't important to you? Do you find yourself finding a new sense of self that doesn't involve letting yourself be defined by other people? Do you feel an abundance in your heart of a new sense of self discovery?

What differences did you notice in your mind and body? What did you notice mentally or emotionally? Ultimately, what do you discover about yourself in who you are and truly want to be or what you want in all aspects of life? While I am not asking you to define your career path, I just want you to only reflect on yourself. This is not about anyone or anything else but finding what's in it for you. By finding our true authentic self, we can then arouse our true desires in money and success or home and family.

After you practice these self care techniques, we can then move onto honing in on our purpose or wealthy endeavors in the next chapter on finding your why ahead.

At the end of the day, there is only one thing that drives us with any enterprise, and that is heart.

The first thing that you need to do in order to be successful at any enterprise is to find what fulfills you in life.

By discovering your true you will be to really find your why.

While the subject of finding your why may seem worn-out, I approach this topic at a much deeper level in helping you to powerfully accumulate massive success and is the most crucial step on your wealth path.

KEY TAKEAWAYS:

- One cannot find success with any career path or business enterprise if their only goal is to chase after money.

- Chasing after the wrong things for the wrong reasons can have us feeling empty inside.

- One can find the motivation we seek by arousing our true self through love and self care.

- Self care is comprised of doing a bunch of wholesome activities that can then arouse peace in our mind, heart and soul which can then bring answers to our authentic selves.

- It is through this portal of finding your true self that you will work at the things that can make you wealthy.
- It is through the power of finding our why that will hone in on seeking our luxurious lifestyle.

*One can embark on these self love and self care activities for any duration of time but we start with the seven day period as most people may get overwhelmed with longer periods of time. Start with the seven day minimum to take it upon yourself to do one self care activity per day for ten to thirty minutes per day, even if it's just journaling your thoughts and feelings from that day.

Jot down any self discoveries you come across with your daily self care activities:

What do you discover about you as to why you aren't pursuing certain get rich paths? What sorts of vocations do you find yourself desiring instead? By doing these activities, what do you discover about what you do or don't want to do and who you do or don't want to be? What would you enjoy doing most in life that is not related to money?

Jot these thoughts down here:

FINDING YOUR DRIVE TO BRING FORTUNE

"The two most important days in your life are the day you were born and the day you find out why."

–Mark Twain

It is now toward the end of your maze to your fortune that you come across the last golden key in finding your true why that you must conquer.

As some of the most famous people have said, finding your why will be one of the most crucial steps you will take in finding your wealthy success. However, I take this exercise of finding your why from a much different approach to help attract wealth to you ahead. Why is this step in amassing wealth so important? Because you will not find the passion and drive to hustle that real estate or day trading get rich system if you cannot find your why in doing it.

Let's take Alexa as an example. Alexa is a friend of mine who came home from work everyday learning the ropes of real estate. No matter how much time she spent delving into her curiosity at these get rich systems, she still found herself letting these ideas and informational books and software pile up in a corner of her house to never touch them. What was holding her back from taking action on these promises to make her rich with these types of systems? Alexa's problem was that she was not finding her passion or purpose in doing them, or her why and her true what's in it for me in doing them. While I can relate with Alexa, it wasn't until I drilled down on my why that I finally found what things I had the passion and drive to aspire at that would bring my real fortunes. I therefore present my secret on how I found my why in my wealth path.

When finding what our why is, you will first start by asking yourself who do you want to be and what do you want to do and why? In extension to this, you can ask yourself a further series of any questions you want such as why do you want to go to college? Why do you want to work where you do? Why do you want to be healthier? Why do you want to run that triathlon? Why do you want a family? Why do you want more money? And why do you want to live where you do amongst many other questions involving all aspects of your life.

Go ahead and think of some lifestyle questions you can ask yourself just like these or any others you can think of and jot them down now:

_____

_____

_____

Remember that these first questions you will ask yourself are only basic in regards to various aspects of your life in home, family, health, and career.

Next, we will then embark on honing in on specific goals and desires that have to do with money or achievements. We will start by asking questions that led you to this book such as the following:

- Why are you reading this book?

- What are you looking for in wealth and personal wealth?

- What are your money goals?

- How wealthy do you want to become and why?

- Are you looking for financial freedom or time freedom, to travel more, get out of debt, support your family, or finding your next job, or looking to buy your dream car and home?

Write down your thoughts on these questions as well as any other thoughts or feelings that come to you such as I have no desire to work at my job anymore and why (or why do I work at a job that I hate so much)?

Quickly write the answers to these questions now:

_____

_____

_____

_____

Once you reflect on these questions, we will then chose a specific goal or life aspect and what your why is on that specific thing (such as I want to get rich with real estate or I want more money or I want to move to the beach or I want to buy my dream car and dream home or I want to pay off debt, retire early and why?)

Now go ahead and reflect on your answers to these questions and jot down what you discover about yourself and what your why is:

After writing down these why's for career and family or life passions, we will now put a twist on digging deeper into your why by going over what your why is not.

Wait, why are we talking about what it's not?

Because when you think you know why you are doing something, you can discover that you are doing the wrong things for the wrong reasons. Additionally, wanting to make a lot of money just so that we can buy big fancy cars and homes is not what motivates us if we have no passion for what we're doing to get there.

Whenever you find yourself confused over any matter, I ask you to really dig deep into what your why is or is not. I almost went to get a college master's degree until I started challenging why I was doing it. When I realized that I only wanted to get a master's degree so that I could feel important, I decided that I was doing it for the wrong reason- to just feel important.

Surprisingly, these are not reasons that motivate us in pursuing any wealth path.

Bluntly spoken - finding your why is not about having a lot of money, buying mansions and yachts, or retiring in the Bahamas. Finding your why is also not about supporting your family, getting out of debt, or getting out of that job you hate so much. Why? Because in the end these are very empty things that don't drive you to work at your ambitions or endeavors when those ambitions and endeavors are there to simply make you money. I know from experience! No matter how much these business enterprises promised to make me filthy rich, I had no desire in pursuing them when I couldn't find the pure passion and drive in pursuing them.

When it comes to the question of finding your why, what we need to do instead is answer the question of what excites you and why it excites you. So when you are trying to answer the question of "Why", you are looking at what is called your internal make-up.

Your internal make-up is what naturally drives you and what you are naturally attracted to. There is no rhyme or reason at all as to why you naturally like what you do. For example, we can't answer the question of why blue is your favorite color and we can't answer the question of why you are attracted to who you are. At the end of the day, you are just simply attracted to who or what you are. There can be many different reasons as to why you are excited about what you are. For example, maybe you are excited about going to school because it makes you feel accomplished or important. Maybe you have a burning passion for what you study and you cannot stop obsessing over it. Maybe all you care about is living a care free life?

So in really drilling down your internal make up, we can embark on the following three tasks:

1. Finding what excites you (what your burning passion is).

2. Finding why it excites you (does it give you fulfillment, make you feel good inside, or something you care about).

3. You can't stop doing it or desiring it! (a chosen ambition of yours).

These are the important steps that you need to take in determining your why and therefore determining your success and then determining what you are going to do for a living. These things can also define how you will change as a person, where you will work or live, who will be in your life and what activities you do.

What is your burning passion and why? It doesn't have to be too complicated. You should already know what you like or are meant to do.

Chances are, you are already doing what you are passionate about in some capacity or you know what you are passionate about and you can realign that with your career and lifestyle.

In answering your own questions to the three steps above, you can simply let the answers come to you naturally on their own or write down some answers as to what you think these are and why and then write a one sentence recap as to what your burning passion is and why.

For example:

I started out by asking myself what makes me burn? The answer was that I wanted to be an author. This subject mattered to me more than anything in the world. I then brainstormed what else I had burning passion for and came up with helping people. And how do I help people? By helping them to turn into giants, helping them to find themselves, helping them to find what they are passionate about, so that they can live their lives to the fullest. This turned into a love for inspiring people. And Why? I feel like I am helping people and I love to help people feel good while inspiring them on their dreams. But why does this make my heart explode and why do I enjoy doing it through writings?

I don't know why and I don't care why. It is what I love.

Maybe I do it because it is my internal make-up. This is simply what I love and what excites me.

One sentence recap:

My burning passion and desire is to inspire people by helping them to do what they love by teaching through books.

Why? Because this is simply what makes my heart explode inside.

In deriving your why, there is absolutely nothing that determines why you love what you do or what motivates you.

We don't know what excites us and we don't know why. We naturally are who we are.

In finding your burning passion for what excites you or motivates you, start by asking the following basic questions:

1. What is your favorite color? Why?

2. What excites you? Why?

3. What do you want to do for a living and why?

4. Where do you want to live?

5. What lifestyle do you want to have?

6. Why does this burning passion or job that you want to do excite you? Is it simply what makes your heart burn? Does it make you feel fulfilled? Does it make you feel important? Does it make you feel like you are helping people? Does it challenge your brain? Does it allow you to be free to go wherever you want? Or it is just natural to you?

Are you doing it for money or for you?

_____

_____

After answering these questions, write a one sentence recap of what you like to do and why?

_____

_____

By answering these questions, you will hone in on the what's in it for you in hustling your passion or getting rid of toxic side businesses that are not enterprising you so that you can find the right path that will. It wasn't until I was doing it for me and not for the money that I found my true success.

As a final quick exercise, ask yourself what you imagine your life to be and what you need to do to get there whether it's selling your home and moving and taking on a new career somewhere. If you don't think these things are possible, then what's stopping you?

By finding your why, you can then dive into the final formula to obtain your biggest asset ahead.

🔑 KEY TAKEAWAYS:

- Finding the motivation and drive to aspire at any ambition is about finding your why or what's in it for you.

- Finding your why is not about being rich so that you can buy your dream cars or dream homes, getting out of debt or retiring because aspiring for the soul purpose of money can leave you feeling empty inside.

- You can find your true why or what's in it for you by figuring out what your why is not and then determining your burning passion for you in your internal make-up.

- By finding your true passion first, money and wealth can follow you.

HOW MUCH SHOULD YOU SPEND ON AN EDUCATION OR WEALTH SYSTEM?

In this chapter: $50,000-$100,000 in savings for you

Once you become rich and savvy with a business, it would be more reasonable for you to drop a million dollars into a business (with advice from financial advisors, lawyers, and business consultants), however, when first starting out, your goal is to spend as little amount of money as possible on any business investment.

Based off of my experience and what I know, it is too expensive to spend even $9.99 a month on a product if you don't know what you are doing. Why? Because you will become victim to the whirlwind of destruction in draining important savings to you. You think I'm joking over such a small fee but if you pay into several of these subscriptions over a 3-5 year span, you can see thousands of dollars disappear from underneath you.

You should not consider paying into any automated systems or third party services until after you have found a capitalist to invest in those services and the business has gained an income from a set of customers.

Remember that the golden formula is to hustle first, find investors or lenders to back you, and then to invest your hard earned money to expand your business as necessary. What this golden formula is saying is that you need to prove a wealth system and get other people's money to help you before you pay into these systems.

Of course it is ok to spend a little bit of up front money for automation services, however, the idea is to sign up with services that have no or as much low cost and up front fees or subscriptions as possible. Additionally, the other idea is to try to get into something where you can get capital from partners or small personal loans* that you can pay back. But let's say that you do get into a business and you really do have to spend some money to get it to launch, or you need to pay for an education program. How much should you spend and how much is too much? The answer to this isn't really that clear and it really depends on what you get involved in. I have spent $40,000 on my education and various business enterprises. Would I recommend that? I cannot recommend how much money anyone should or should not spend on education or business platforms as everyone's journey is going to be different and you can learn a lot from anything you do. However, there are a few parameters and guidelines I can suggest on how much you should spend on anything (besides next to zero), based off of my experience:

Certificate programs: You can get many in demand certificates for as little as ten dollars and some from more reputable schools for as little as $50- $1000.00. These amounts are based on the standards of what most people would pay for these programs. Stay away from any certificate that costs $1999.00 or more until you have thoroughly researched everything you need to do to make your business profitable as well as the monthly expenses involved of running a business that certificate program claims to help you launch.**

If you are going to spend a lot of money on any education platform such as online degrees, you should thoroughly research job prospects and what type of return on investment you can get from it. It's always advisable to speak with recruiters on which certificate programs are best to invest into for a career track or to see if they can pay you back.

Real estate: up to $1000.00. You can get a commercial loan and you can partner with people who will put in the capital if you do a lot of the work. The $1000.00 might be needed for legal fees or automation services, although the idea is to get the loan and the capitalist to cover all up front investments and costs.

Digital service such as a blog or marketing services: Free web hosting and digital integration through Mailchimp.com until you can gain traction and your first paycheck.

Book writing: I would not spend more than $1000.00 for editing, proofreading, copywriting, ghostwriting, self publishing, and marketing. Why? Because you have no idea if your book is going to sell. If you can, take a few English composition courses, write your book, and have it line edited. If your book takes off, then maybe consider doing a full edit on it at that point. It is common for author's to do several edits on their manuscripts even after they have sold a thousand copies.

Domains: use free webhosting services that provide free domains until you gain traction with a business. If you do buy a cheap .88 cents domain, use caution and avoid .xyz domains as most computer engines are programmed to avoid these in search engines as they are usually bought up by scammers.

You can see that there is a trend here that you should not spend more than $1000.00 on any business enterprise or education program in a given year or as free as possible, however, if you do spend that kind of money, be very reserved about what you spend it on. It doesn't take much to lose out on fifty to one hundred thousand dollars on business systems that may never launch or could fail within the first year of business.

Oh and one more thing: don't give a dime to any patent or idea buying companies for your new ideas or inventions as most of these are scams. The only people you should pitch your big start up ideas to are the big reputable venture capitalists of silicone valley as only 0.05% of ideas are bought by these people. A reputable venture capitalist will never ask for your up front money when pitching your idea to them. Which also reminds me, I wouldn't spend $150 a month for someone to build a social media platform for me unless I had the one unicorn invention and built traction with it first.

Rather than dumping your money into any of these above mentioned systems, the most realistic thing you can do is to get a side job*** or take on overtime at an hourly job and to spend your money on wealth management to amass your wealth to you.

A few hundred to a few thousand dollars on legitimate people who do real things of financial value such as good wealth manager, a tax or real estate lawyer, and a real estate agent will do. By paying fees into these types of professionals, you can find a reverse whirlwind of massive savings and preservation of $100,000.00 in front of you.

KEY TAKEAWAYS:

- Spending even $9.99 a month can be too expensive in money draining subscriptions and systems.

- One should follow the golden formula to hustle and prove a wealth system before surrendering any money on it.

- You should not spend more than $1000.00 on any certificates or other opportunities until you know how lucrative it will be for you.

- It would be more beneficial to spend your money on wealth managers, lawyers, and consultants who can enterprise you.

*Be careful when seeking loans to start any business and never do so without receiving consult from a lawyer and having a strong positive outlook on the business as banks can use your house as collateral against the loan!

**A lot of programs bait you in that you can make thousands of dollars a month with their programs and systems without divulging all of the costs involved in advertising, marketing, legal costs, web and web hosting services, and rental space at an office somewhere, as well as subscriptions to use their proprietary information which can also cost as much as $200 a month. Ecommerce can also involve paying thousands of dollars a month for dropshipping and other integrations to sell products. Be sure to look into all of these costs before buying into any program that promises to make you a lot of money.

***A word of caution on side hustles:

As the economy continues to tighten, more people may find themselves working for tips at part time jobs and side hustles. A few of these types of jobs that have become popular include delivery and ride share services. Although these jobs can bring in good side income, please be aware of the risks in doing them. These types of jobs are placed in one of the top ten most dangerous jobs due to traffic accidents, robberies, and assaults. So if you look into any of these types of side hustles, be sure to do so with extreme caution in the cities and neighborhoods you chose to serve and to have the most auto insurance coverage that you need including commercial or business use vehicle packages to you. As ignorant as any of us want to be that accidents never happen to us, you'll find teenage drivers who may blow a stop sign in front of you.

YOUR BIGGEST ASSET AND THE WORST FINANCIAL MOVE YOU CAN MAKE

"An investment in knowledge pays the best interest."

–Benjamin Franklin

Robert Kiyosaki states in some of his education books and trainings that some of the worst financial mistakes one can make are buying a home and cars which he refers to as liabilities rather than assets.

The book titled "The Millionaire Next door" also talks about how "smart" millionaires are able to keep their wealth by being conservative with the types of cars that they buy.

So what is the worst financial mistake you can make? Is it the investments you chose? The house you buy? The debt you go into? Shopping sprees? Student loans? I think this is a very debatable question, but I will go over what I think are some of the biggest financial mistakes that you can make which are not having multiple income streams and not obtaining your biggest asset.

In a day and age of rising inflation and housing costs, a regular 9-5 job and a retirement plan isn't going to do it for us anymore. In order to gain my wealth, I personally had to work my butt off in all of these various active and passive income streams mentioned in this book. Did these things actually make me wealthy? Heck no. But did they allow me to become wealthy? Pursuing all of these things allowed me the savings and cash flow that I needed in order to find wealth through accredited high net worth early investments in fintech* to explode my snowball of wealth further.

But it wasn't only these systems I built in active and passive income that helped me to do so.

As important as wealth management and building income streams will be to your overall wealthfolio, we will now go over obtaining your biggest asset in creating cash flow and passive income for you. An asset by the way is anything that you own that can bring economic value or be converted into cash and bring cash flow to you.

While you might think you know what your biggest asset is, it certainly isn't your primary residential home if you are in over your head with your mortgage and are not collecting rental income on the debt of your home loan. Your biggest assets in accumulating wealth are not even material or in that of real estate at all.

Are you ready for it? Your biggest assets in accumulated wealth is not physical, but rather non physical as we discussed in the tale of the highest paid people in converting valuable intangible things into tangible results for people and falls under the following wealth formula:

Your Biggest Asset = ((Education + Hustle + Cash Flow(savings and income) – Debt) ^ Time = Wealth Accumulation

Your biggest asset is the sum of your education, hard work, and cash flow, minus all of your debt, multiplied by the power of time which will determine your total wealth accumulation ahead of you.

Education is by far one of the biggest assets you can ever own that you can convert into cash. How do I know? Think of all of the wealthiest people who have education in engineering, technology, and other subjects that make them massively wealthy. Even if some of the wealthiest billionaires didn't finish school, they still get the education they need to become prodigies in their fields. Education can also be comprised of learning any valuable knowledge that can make you wealthy if you know how to sell it to masses of people.

In referring to the power of time, I go back to your disciplined motivation to hustle everyday for as long as it takes to bring fortune to you.

Even universities such as the University of California at Berkeley recognize that savings, work ethic, and hustle can bring a wealth of income to you in which you can convert active income into passive income for you as the following chart shows:

Active Income   **Assets**

Education   cash flow and income streams

Hustle

So this is where the formula of passion, action, education, times intensity (hard work and hustle) comes in to enterprise you. You must have severe passion in anything you do to keep working at it and gaining the education you need to enterprise it and intensifying that hard work over a matter of time to bring wealth to you.

One of the other biggest assets that will accumulate your wealthfolio will be in your massive savings to you.

Wealth management not only involves savings in protecting your money in insurance and hidden fees or avoiding debt, but also being thrifty in spending money on furniture and clothes as I did over a twenty year span of my lifetime. In order to amass my wealth, I bought most of my wardrobe at thrift stores and took in used furniture from friends and family with the mindset that these habits would make me rich someday. I didn't actually know how real this was until one day I only had literally one day to put a minimum of $50,000 into a private investment with a potential for massive return. If you knew that you can become wealthy someday by living this frugally, would you do it? I'm glad I did and I wouldn't change it for the world today, because now I'm on my way to have the life that 99% of people will never get to see.

Being thrifty in the things you buy from cars and homes, cell phones and attire over a ten or twenty year time span will be one of the most powerful things you can do in accumulating wealth for you.

As a case in point, what do you think is the difference between me and a past co-worker who I will call Billy? Billy and I were both working at the same part time job making minimum wage plus tips, and both driving older white sedans. Billy was a new hire and showed up to work flaunting his brand new $1500.00 trendy cell phone while I was coming into work everyday with my brand new $234.00 un-trendy but competitively made cell phone with all of the same specs as his. But the financial difference between us was not $1266.00. The financial difference was $100,000.00 between us! Billy had spent weeks griping about how he was negative $200.00 in his bank account while turning down extra hours and shifts and spending over a thousand dollars on a new phone whereas I had a fat bank account from not having to have expensive things in life and taking on extra shifts at work. It is similar to the principles that are taught in the think and grow rich book. Those who have money are those who are more disciplined with money.

Preach aside, one cannot fully grasp what the power of savings on various expenses can do for you until you sit down with a piece of paper and do the math. Think about it. If you can save $40.00 a month by switching to a different cell phone carrier, that comes out to $480.00 a year or $4800.00 in ten years. You can find yourself saving as much as $25,000 in ten years by cutting all of your various bills in half wherever possible, and saving tens of thousands of dollars by using realtors who will work for you with lower commission rates. What can an extra twenty five grand do for you in ten years? This is extra money that you can put into real estate or investment opportunities. So whenever experts preach to sit down with a piece of paper and calculate where you can cut expenses, what they really mean is that this one exercise alone can potentially mean the difference of hundreds of thousands of dollars and lucrative opportunities that you can get into down the road with your extra savings for you.

Let's think of another easy money principle. What do you think the difference is between a $1.00 item and a $5.00 item, assuming that they are the same product of equal value? This item can be anything you want from food items to cosmetics, shampoo, cleaning supplies, or anything that costs between one and five dollars. In this case we will use a bottle of soap because everyone buys it. We will assume that for the purposes of this exercise, that the two bottles of soap are equal in value- size and quality of the product. Assuming everything else is the same, the difference between the two bottles of soap- one costing $1.00 and the other costing $5.00 is not a $4.00 difference! In reality, there is a 500% difference between them. In order to really see the true difference in the price of these two items over time, we can either multiply the cost of buying these items every time we buy them over a one year to ten year time frame, or we can change the common denominator by multiplying them by 100. So to see the real difference of what you are spending on these two items, think of the $1.00 value as actually $100 and the $5.00 item as $500.00. The true difference between these two items is really $400.00 when you leverage it with time- how often you have to buy them- or- when combined with everything else you have to buy.

If you spend $1.00 on something everyday, that comes out to $365.00 a year on spending of that item. But if you chose to buy the more expensive $5.00 item everyday, that comes out to $1825.00 in yearly spending on a comparable item, a $1460 difference! Even more so, when you combine these savings with the hundreds of items you have to buy each time you shop or with your cell phone carrier and auto insurance savings among others, you are easily saving $10,000 - $50,000 in one year alone! So the next time you comparison shop on any two items, change the value from one to one hundred. Anything that is $2.00 is actually $200.00, 3.00 is $300.00, $4.00 is $400.00, and then you will start to see the real difference of what you are spending between any two items because I can assure you it is not just the three or five dollar difference that you are seeing!

A few more golden nuggets for you:

One of the most important things you can do for your wealthfolio is to get rid of everything that is distracting you and narrowing your goals in order to accumulate your wealth further.

As preachy and cliché as this may seem, I didn't see success without narrowing my goal to one path that would lead me to massive success. This is one step that any rich entrepreneur takes very seriously. As the saying goes,

"The person attempting to travel two roads at once will get nowhere…" –Xunzi

So now what do I really mean by narrowing your goals to one path that will lead you to massive success?

Have you ever come across someone's professional online profile or resume in which they had five different entrepreneurial jobs or a career portfolio of ten different trades that they currently doing at the same time. I see this all the time, and while these people want to ignore my suggestions to narrow their focus to only one thing, they remain unsuccessful in making huge profits at any of them.

A smart and proven entrepreneur doesn't get rich by being the jack of all trades or by selling everything under the sun. A smart and proven entrepreneur remains intensively focused on one and only path that will make him rich. A smart entrepreneur knows exactly what he is doing and gives all of his attention to the one enterprise that will make him explosively wealthy, rather than trying to sell ten completely unrelated products and services under the same brand.

So why would focusing on one thing lead to massive success? There are two reasons why. First of all, if you get distracted ten different ways then you will not put all of the attention, time, and energy that is needed into one thing to make it successful. The second reason is that if you do not focus on one product or service then customers are going to reject you. What exact product or service are you providing to me? I am going to go to a medical doctor who is a professional in their field and who will get me back to health but I lack interest in someone who is trying to sell a mix of too many unrelated things at once spanning from educational products in finance and career along with clothing and coffee (yes, I actually ran into a company who was selling all of these things and they are struggling to make sales as of this writing). Additionally, I am not going to trust someone who is not an expert in their field. I am going to go directly to the one source that adds value and solves a specific problem or sells a specific product.

More so, if you focus on real estate one day and blogging another day and book writing the third day and trying to pitch your new social media app every other week, you find that all products lack performance which further discourages you. Additionally, investors and venture capitalists will not fund any of your ideas if you have not put the time and energy you need into them to make them gain traction with people. If you want to become that next mega millionaire superstar, then you need to focus on one thing that will make you wealthy and I hope that this information can help to narrow that path for you.

Now don't get confused with rich people who have ten income streams as those are people who built those streams individually before they became wealthy. There is nothing wrong with buying real estate while hustling a job and going to school. I am mostly talking about those who are trying to run too many entrepreneurial businesses at once which is impossible to do. But you can still focus on one career path or business venture while doing all of the other things that you can do in building income streams and savings for you.

While we are talking about narrowing your goals to one thing, it will also be important that you don't try to become a walking encyclopedia by learning everything there is to know about a product or information you are selling as these things will hold you down and keep you from succeeding. A successful entrepreneur will simply get to work while having resources that they can refer to rather than trying to memorize everything. Those who do will find themselves going down the rabbit hole of destruction as they never move forward in their business.

While on the journey to your wealth success, it will be of the essence that you don't let long to-do lists destroy you. When you write such long, complicated to-do lists, they become overwhelming in which you don't do and get distracted by other things that won't enterprise you. The most important thing to do is to take action on the biggest or most important item on your to do list to propel you to massive success. You do this by putting no more than three to-do items on your list at a time in which you may find fortunes come to you.

And One Final Thing: Don't let anyone tell you what you can or cannot do, what you will or will not do. As the saying goes:

The first editor I sent this book to before publishing told me I would not succeed in selling this book in which I'm not going to listen to someone who has no knowledge in finance or wealth management and furthermore is going to send sample edits to me that made me question their education and degree.

I am not intending to slam this person but to rather encourage you to move forward with your goals and accomplishments regardless of any naysayers, because at the end of the day, these people don't know what they are talking about and what is possible within you.

In reality, there is never any guarantee of results with anything that you do and those who do invest in any vehicle whether real estate, fintech, stocks or bonds are gambling with the ebb and flow of the markets.

Additionally, anything that you do in real estate and investments can be risky in which a serendipitous fate of luck can determine your wealth for you.

At one point, Colorado was a goldmine for buying real estate in which many people bought homes in an up and hot selling market only to be subject to having mortgages worth more than their homes once the market pops and home values deflate. I was lucky to buy my home in a down market before prices rose in which I could sell it for a high ticket and make a decent profit.

Was it all risky? Very. And of course I had to remain patient over a twenty year span before I saw my snowball of wealth to manifest for me.

So if it's not that easy to become explosively wealthy with real estate or fintech, how can anyone become wealthy? Most people can do so with the final golden shamrock formula in building income streams through wages patience risk and luck ahead of you.

The golden shamrock formula:

Wages/Hustle	Patience/Faith
Risk	Luck

As none of these investments or wealth strategies are guaranteed to return any money to you, it will be in the massive actions that you take to working your A-S-S off to bring residual income and cash flow to you and consulting qualified advisors to help you. It will be up to you to determine which of the various investment and enterprise wealth strategies you want to pursue that will bring your fortunes to you.

When you need further guidance on this journey, you turn to the Wind Whisperer and your Diary and plug into the mystical powers of the Rustic Golden Tree. Trust in yourself to find the answers in which you will unravel an abundance of knowledge and wisdom within you.

It is with all of this that I wish you the best in all that you do in finding massive savings and wealth to you. As you found in this book, it is anyone who can follow these personal wealth principles who can find savings and fortune ahead of them, but for those who are more serious in amassing fortune, it will be in my next book "Think and Be Rich and the Portal to Online Gold" that will reveal more secrets to you.

🔑 KEY TAKEAWAYS:

- The worst financial move you can make is to not have multiple streams of income and to not obtain your biggest asset.

- Your biggest asset can be summed by a formula consisting of passion, action, education, times intensity (hard work and hustle) multiplied by the power of time.

- The people who find the most success get rid of all distractions and clutter and narrow their wealth career to one thing.

- The final golden formula is wages, patience, risk, and luck.

*There is no guarantee in investing in fintech or any other type of investment no matter what it is and advisors will tell you that fintech and real estate are highly risky. If you want to work with any of these types of investments, it would be of benefit to you to not do so without seeking legal advice and working with qualified brokers to help you.

Additionally, there are qualifications you must meet to become an accredited investor such as sustained income levels with yourself or with a spouse or hold specific financial licenses and therefore it will be on those who work at gaining high wages that will be able to enter into these types of opportunities.

The accredited investor requirements can be located through **https://www.sec.gov**.

Think and Be Rich and the Portal to Financial Gold

www.ingramcontent.com/pod-product-compliance
Lightning Source LLC
Chambersburg PA
CBHW071050090426
42737CB00013B/2310